D0323744

Versus: Reflections of A Sociologist

Versus: Reflections of A Sociologist

BY
HENRY PRATT FAIRCHILD

KENNIKAT PRESS/PORT WASHINGTON, N. Y.

VERSUS: REFLECTIONS OF A SOCIOLOGIST

Reissued in 1969 by Kennikat Press by arrangement
Library of Congress Catalog Card No: 74-86015
SBN 8046-0557-2

Manufactured by Taylor Publishing Company Dallas, Texas

ESSAY AND GENERAL LITERATURE INDEX REPRINT SERIES

BY WAY OF INTRODUCTION

In presenting these collected essays, former students, colleagues and friends of Professor Henry Pratt Fairchild have sought to honor a beloved teacher upon his retirement from academic duties in the Graduate School of New York University. VERSUS, however, is in no sense a tablet to commemorate the past, but is rather a milestone on a continuous road of scholarly, critical analysis of our social behavior. The studies are as effective to-day in illuminating the obscure vistas of public events as they were when first presented. We offer them now for their historical and educational values to an extended classroom.

In common with many other independent thinkers, Professor Fairchild's ideas have frequently aroused opposition as well as commendation. No one, however, has ever doubted his integrity and sincere devotion to the public welfare. He has never spared himself in the interest of our society. To Henry Pratt Fairchild may aptly be applied the words of Emerson, ". . . the great man is he who, in the midst of the crowd, keeps with perfect sweetness the independence of solitude."

The Publication Committee.

FOREWORD

The stimulation of many minds to creative thought and the motivation of many fellow citizens to action in the interest of human welfare are the only social justifications for recognition of an intellectual career through spontaneous action by former students, colleagues and friends. Those of us who have known Henry Pratt Fairchild over the years are delighted that such spontaneous recognition has come to him through this volume of selections from his writings. For us there is no need of a Foreword, although we may take pleasure in an impressionistic recounting of his roles in the communities of interest we share with him. Others who did not have the opportunity of including him among their friends and teachers may find these brief comments on his full life of achievement useful in the understanding of the development of American social theory and practice.

As a personal friend and younger sociological colleague I have been given the privilege of attempting to set forth, but in far too few words, my interpretation of what there is about Dr. Fairchild that has so stimulated his students and associates. His willingness to have the Foreword to this published tribute entrusted to me who is of a divergent though overlapping school of sociological thought reflects the exceptional trait of intellectual democracy evident in all his relations with associates.

Understanding of a man's career must begin with knowledge of the man himself. It is a bit in the nature of a summation of popular estimation of personality that whether in his presence or absence, reference is usually to Hal Fairchild, not to Doctor, Professor or Mr. Fairchild. Mere physical appearance is never without significance in relation to any role of leadership, so reference to his impressive stature and genial appearance may not be omitted. Age is another important although ever changing personal attribute. Hal Fairchild's age is far less evident in his outward appearance and current activities than in his record of accomplishments. His title of Professor Emeritus at New York University is the only evidence that he is now over sixty-five years of age chronologically speaking, but it is difficult for his friends to believe. We are more impressed by his continued multitudinous activities as an author, lecturer and worker in a variety of organizations and movements for the benefit of mankind, and by his inexhaustible geniality, humor, generosity and effective diligence.

Most of those who read this book probably will know the author best as an academician, as a teacher and as a scholar. His academic career has included service at International College in Turkey, and in this country at Doane College, his alma mater, at Bowdoin College, at Yale University, where he received his doctorate, and at New York University, where he was a member of the faculty for twenty-six years and for the latter part of that time Chairman of the Department of Sociology in the Graduate School of Arts and Science. The published results of his research and scholarship are listed elsewhere in this volume, but it may be mentioned here that they include distinguished contributions to the science of society, to materials for teaching, to the popularization of social knowledge and to the persuasive literature for social improvement. A sociologist by formal training and affiliation, much of this writing has been on economic questions and one may suspect some gentle regret that the focus of specialization by chance or choice was not in the latter field. Even so, disciplinary formalities have never stood a chance when they got in the way of his selection of problems and materials for writing or teaching.

Henry Pratt Fairchild the academician may not be appreciated without acquaintance with Henry Pratt Fairchild the leader in social action. Direct concern with human welfare appears in his early staff association with the War Camp Community Service during World War I, the Connecticut State Commission on Child Welfare and the University Settlement of New York. It also has been given tangible expression by his leadership in such voluntary associations as the People's League for Economic Security, the American Commonwealth Political Federation, the Commonwealth Federation of New York, Film Audiences for Democracy, the Birth Control Federation, the American Eugenics Society, the Town Hall Club, and many others. That he has been unstinting of his time and effective in his efforts to mobilize and co-operate with others in social action programs is shown by the fact that he has held the office of president or chairman of all the organizations just listed except one, and he was vice president of that one. It is in point to observe that he has also served as president of the American Sociological Society, the Eastern Sociological Society and the American Population Association, social science organizations in fields furnishing knowledge basic for intelligent social action. It is characteristic of his work for the improvement of social conditions that his approach to social problems consistently has been through the application of social knowledge in the amelioration of social ills.

The selection of Dr. Fairchild's papers here reprinted is his own. They do not represent a cross-section of his total publications, nor is it intended that they should. Each reader of Dr. Fairchild's works naturally retains a recollection of their contributions biased by his own personal interests. As a sociologist, I recall his sociological writings best. As a specialist in the problems of minority peoples, I have been most impressed by his pioneering writings on immigration. Others will think that more should have been included in the field of population, or eugenics, or social theory, and so on. Still others will regret the limited representation of his substantive contributions to social knowledge. The purpose of the selection, however, is to reveal a single thread running through all his publications, his classroom teaching, his public lectures and his active participation in practical affairs. It is fitting that he himself should have the privilege of bringing together those papers which best reveal his lifelong and consistent exposition of the difficult and inevitable choices constantly faced by all mankind. All who read his modest introduction following this Foreword must agree with this decision.

The selections which reveal this thread of philosophic continuity reveal other things as well. They reveal a man deeply and sincerely devoted to the advancement of mankind as a whole. They reveal a scholar not content with the scholarship of the ivory tower. They reveal a leader fearless of the sanctions of orthodoxy in any of its forms, whether academic or communal. They reveal a teacher and a leader who in spite of firm convictions is neither pedantic nor dogmatic, but rather an educator who uses facts and his own interpretations to make others think and act for themselves. These are the qualities which have made me, along with countless others, his appreciative informal student.

Donald Young

New York

CONTENTS

INTRODUCTION

Many years ago I entered Switzerland from Italy by way of the railroad that includes at its summit the famous St. Gotthard tunnel. It was a memorable and exciting experience. The scenery was breath-taking. The road twisted and turned in a seemingly haphazard pattern, plunging through the spur of a mountain here, crossing to the other side of a chasm there, and occasionally gaining altitude by boring into the heart of the mountain itself in a great spiral and coming out almost directly above where it went in. I found myself wondering, "How on earth did they ever know where to put this railroad? How could they decide that one valley was better than another, where to locate a bridge, and when to accept the huge cost of a tunnel?"

Later on I saw an inclusive relief map of the whole region, and in a flash my question was answered. The railroad was laid out along the only major line where it could have been. Seen in the large it was clear as crystal that the broad outline of the project was determined by nature itself, and the features that had attracted my attention from the car window were merely minor details of the man-made solution.

In like manner, looking back over long years of following the devious path of human experience and pondering upon its sometimes dramatic, sometimes expensive, but always interesting incidents, I have come to see that much of human destiny is shaped by broad and inescapable features of the cosmos itself. I realize too that my own reflections, and my own efforts to interpret the meaning of life, have been shaped according to certain basic laws and principles of which I was by no means fully conscious at the moment. Viewed in the wide perspective of time, certain major configurations of thought stand out boldly, and I now realize that many of the reflections and interpretations to which I have given expression are in essence merely manifestations of great fundamentals.

One of these all-encompassing truths has to do with the essential tragedy of choice which besets the human individual from the cradle to the grave. This is not the kind of alternative ordinarily postulated in ethical and philosophical writings — the choice between good and evil. Rather is it the necessity on many occasions of making an inevitable choice between two mutually exclusive goods, or between two evils which are so related that if one escapes the former he must inevitably fall victim to the latter. The essay in which I first set forth publicly my realization of this fateful law appears as the opening selection in this volume. Many of those that follow represent analyses of specific subjects written before I had reached the realization of the immanent character of the central theme. Viewed in retrospect, they seem to present a consistent development of interpretation, and as such it is my humble hope that they may be of some service to others in helping to understand their own particular problems and perplexities.

H. P. F.

EDITORIAL PREFACE

In planning this volume the question naturally and inevitably arose as to whether an effort should be made to revise statements appearing in the present tense so as to bring them into conformity with the contemporary scene at the time of publication of the book. After much deliberation, but with no demur, the decision was reached to leave each essay exactly as it was printed.

The reasons for this are obvious. They fall into two main classes. In the first place so many of the discussions, while dealing with enduring fundamentals, are timely in character that to carry the revisionary process to its ultimate conclusion would leave the original texts hopelessly mangled. Second, as sociological treatises, these articles contain many interpretations and predictions, the validity of which can be tested, and the interest in them enhanced, by projecting them from the time they were written against the cold facts of 1950.

To aid the reader in getting this chronological orientation the date of original publication is appended as a foot-note at the beginning of each essay.

Versus: Reflections of A Sociologist

1

BUT YOU CAN'T HAVE BOTH

Written in 1934

Once to every man and nation
Comes the moment to decide.
In the strife of truth with falsehood,
For the good or evil side.

So RUNS the orthodox doctrine. In the traditional and conventional concepts of dualism the antithesis of life is characteristically presented as a conflict between Good and Evil, a choice between Light and Darkness, Right and Wrong. Ormuzd and Ahriman, God and Satan, are represented as the two forces whose contention for the mastery of the human spirit causes so much perplexity, bitterness, and struggle. We are led to believe that it is the persistent and multifarious necessity of choosing between Good and Bad, Duty and Pleasure, Virtue and Vice that creates the problems of human life and causes the bulk of unhappiness and misery.

This is a gross and palpable error. Not that cases of discomfort arising from this type of choice are not numerous and familiar. But they are of relatively slight gravity and constitute only a minor portion of the total burden of wretchedness.

The reason is that choices of this kind, bothersome as they are, never create insoluble problems or impose insuperable obstacles. The terms of such a choice are usually, in the very nature of the case, comparatively clear. On the one hand is Good, on the other Evil. Those who choose to choose Good, choose Good, and are happy in their choice.

Those who choose to choose Evil, choose Evil, and are equally happy in their choice. If in general, and in the long run, human happiness is better promoted by the predominant choice of Good rather than Evil, man in his age-long experience is likely to find it out and to act accordingly. This is, indeed, necessarily so. For what is Good except that which man, by long practice in choosing, has found to be conducive to his happiness? If there were only one great, inclusive Good or only one specific Good accessible at a time, man would eventually learn to recognize it, and would have no excuse for suffering. Truth would be synonymous with the distinction between Good and Evil, and it could be accurately said, "Know the truth, and the truth shall make you free." There would then be some justification for the doctrine, so pathetically and disastrously cherished among Western democratic peoples, that in education is to be found the comprehensive and adequate solution for all human problems, the remedy for every kind of ill.

But when one faces the facts of mundane existence squarely he discovers that the really devastating antithesis of life is found, not in the choice between Good and Evil, but in the perennially recurring and inescapable necessity of choosing between two goods or between two evils. This is the very essence of tragedy, and it is the universality of situations of this kind that makes life on this planet essentially tragic. It is this type of antithesis that creates insoluble problems and, therefore, produces unavoidable and perpetual distress. Life teems with conditions and relationships in which we are confronted with two good alternatives, perhaps equally good, on such terms that if we seize the one we must forego the other, or we are faced with two evils that are so related that in order to escape one we must necessarily submit to the other. It is in consequence of recurrent dilemmas of this sort that human existence is never wholly happy, but always tainted with misery, regret, and a heavy burden of frustration.

One may slide from the sublime to the ridiculous and back again and find innumerable illustrations all along the way. Any charming young debutante can supply you with plenty of cases. While her fingertips are still tingling with the thrill of reading the note from her friend Jim, the promising young playwright, inviting her to attend the opening night of his first Broadway venture, the telephone rings and there is Tom's voice asking her to go with him to the Yale Prom. Alas! they come on the same evening. Five or six years ago, strange as it may now seem, many a young man fresh from college was faced with the necessity of choosing between two good jobs. Should he step into the place in his father's factory that had been held for him during all the years of his education, and enter upon a smooth and secure (as it seemed then) pathway to financial prominence and prosperity, or should he accept the offer that so surprisingly had come to him from a little Western college, and devote himself to the teaching of English literature that his soul loved?

A similar decision, immeasurably more momentous in character, confronted the American nation in 1917. We were intrinsically a peaceloving people. We had just elected a President on the ground that "He kept us out of war." We were riding on the crest of the wave of prosperity through our lucrative trade with the combatant nations across the water. The ostensible issues at stake in Europe were not ours. It seemed that we had nothing to gain and all to lose by entering the conflict. And then we woke up to discover that the implacable march of events had brought us face to face with a decision. The activities of the Central Powers were threatening us with national humiliation and possible invasion, spoliation, and subjection. Our only means of protection was war. We had to choose, but the choice was between two evils. The unavoidable price for escape from one evil was casting ourselves irrevocably into the other.

It is inherent in human nature to rebel against this aspect of destiny. We naturally want all the good things that we recognize as being within our reach and we want to escape all the evils that we know to be intrinsically avoidable. To find that we are prevented from having one good only by our insistence on having another good irks us profoundly. To realize that the only reason why one evil is inflicted upon us is our determination to dodge another evil arouses our deepest resentment.

Only the other day, for example, a man who has charge of the arrangement of a very important radio program made the following observation, "The trouble with my comedian is that he wants to give a regular vaudeville sketch and fill a spot in a crowded radio 'hour' at the same time. I point out to him that he is allowed precisely three minutes, and his script runs to four and a half minutes. He says, 'What can we do about it? It's swell stuff.' I say, 'Well, we'll have to cut out this gag and this one and that one.' He protests vehemently, 'You can't do that—those are my best lines.' 'All right,' I say, 'then we'll cut out this one and that.' 'Oh!' he says,'you can't do that. It's all good.' He flies into an emotional tempest, wasting his nervous energy and mine, and of course finally has to submit to the three-minute limit."

We are all like that. We are inveterately disposed to eat our cake and have it too. Consequently we refuse to resign ourselves to the situation and calmly to choose one good in gratitude that it is good, or to select one evil, thankful that it is not two. Instead, we close our eyes and rush madly in pursuit of two contradictory goods or persist in kicking stubbornly against two sets of pricks, one of which—but only one, if we would but choose—is unavoidable.

It is a rarely philosophic soul who can make a choice and then cast the other alternative forever into the limbo of forgotten things. Most of us have mnemonic picture galleries through which we forever wander, gazing dolefully on the black-framed and crepe-shrouded mementos of the joys we might have had "if only . . ." The climax of gloomy remorse is reached when, as so frequently happens, the event proves that our choice was wrong. The play to which you finally decided to go was postponed on account of a stage-hands' strike, while Tom fell in love with the girl that he took to the Prom in your place and married her. Father's business, with which you cast in your lot, failed, while the insignificant little college got a huge bequest, and the young assistant professor of English language and literature receives a salary of five thousand dollars.

> For of all sad words of tongue or pen,
> The saddest are these: "It might have been!"

Even when two incompatible goods are of uneven value, we are loath to give up the lesser for the sake of the greater, especially if it is one that we have long enjoyed. The records of divorce courts tell only a part of the tale, and the term "incompatibility" covers a multitude of things. But we may be sure that to them are brought the wrecks of many a marriage that might have been happy except for the unwillingness of one or the other of the parties, or both, to relinquish celibate self-determination as the inescapable price of connubial comfort. Sometimes reluctance to bow to the inevitable expresses itself in an attempt at compromise, and the "busy evenings at the office" or the "conferences out of town" become more and more frequent. In other cases the renunciation is made completely, but not cheerfully; the feeling of regret is cherished, and the marital partner serves more and more as a reminder of the things that used to be.

A shrewd appreciation of this reality led Count Keyserling, in his introductory chapter to "The Book of Marriage", to observe that the real cause of the failure of marriage in Western lands is that we expect it to be happy. If we could only learn to contemplate marriage, not as an instrument of unalloyed bliss, but as a means to the realization of personality, with all the suffering and sacrifice that that involves, we should be better prepared to reap its full rewards.

II

The conditions out of which arise the various phases of the great antithesis inhere in different departments of human life upon this finite globe. Some of them are determined by natural forces or cosmic qualities over which man has no control. Others are inherent in what we call "human nature." Some are a combination of both. Perhaps the most influential, the most universal, and the most devastating is the implacable conflict between the two basic impulses, the two fundamental desires, of mankind—hunger and love. This antithesis is by no means exclusively human, but is a feature of all organic life, and, indeed, owes its unequalled power for misery to its firm entrenchment in the very nature of things. Its character, and its mode of operation, can best be understood by considering first the lower forms of life.

It has been frequently observed, by poets and others, that Nature's chief concern is for the perpetuation of each of the species that she has created. To this end, she has equipped her creatures with a prodigious capacity for multiplication, backed up by that domineering urge to mate that we generalize under the name of love. The results are overwhelming. The rates of reproduction, particularly in the lower levels of organic life, stagger the imagination when first encountered. Of one minute organism it is said that, if left to itself, a single individual would in thirty days form a mass a million times the size of the sun. A moderate example is furnished by the oyster, the female of which lays on the average sixteen million eggs a year. At this rate, a single male and female would in five years produce a mass of oysters—the great-

great-grandchildren of the original pair—eight times the size of the earth. As we ascend the scale of evolution the birth rate becomes progressively smaller until, in such species as the lion and the elephant, it reaches a very moderate figure. But a high rate of reproduction would not be necessary to attain stupendous totals in a short time if all the offspring survived. For the reproduction of a species is a matter of geometrical progression. The simple fact is that there is not a species in existence that does not multiply fast enough to overflow the earth in a very few generations, if there were nothing to stop it.

What does stop it?

The basic demand that the individual organism makes of Nature, aside from sheer standing-room, is food. This food all comes from the earth's crust, either directly as in the case of plants, or at one or more removes as in the case of animals. The crust of the earth is composed of some ninety-odd elements, about a dozen of which are utilized in the formation of organic tissues. These food elements exist in absolutely limited amounts and stable quantities. In other words, the amount of food in the world is a fixed quantity. And if the amount of food is limited, the amount of life is also limited. Hence arises Nature's great, ironic joke. She invites to her banquet literally infinite numbers of her creatures and then places before them a restricted and unalterable amount of nourishment. There can be only one outcome—the death of the overwhelming majority, and no continuing increase whatever. Such is Nature's method of accomplishing her great end. The more one studies Nature, the more he is impressed with the extent to which her processes consist of various forms of slaughter.

Man, the animal, started his career subject to the same rigorous regimen. Like the other creatures about him, he brought into the world, generation after generation, offspring who, in the nature of the case, were destined to be his most dangerous competitors. The primary relation between parents and offspring is one of implacable hostility and competition. The maple tree, standing alone in the meadow, season after season surrounds itself with myriad offspring, all of whom it proceeds to choke in infancy. If, by good fortune, one or two saplings manage to survive and grow into sturdy trees, they become the most dangerous enemies of the parent, which eventually in the years of its decrepitude they crowd to destruction. Man is no exception. The pristine enmity between parents and children has been a prominent factor in human affairs. The fact that, in the face of this inherent conflict, the higher forms of animal life, including man, should have developed a real parental and filial bond of affection, devotion, and self-sacrifice is one of the most impressive phenomena of evolution. The combination of these two forces has produced some widespread and persistent cultural forms. Infanticide is a well-known and extensive expression of enmity, which has by no means died out even in supposedly civilized countries. The killing of the old by the young is less conspicuous—partly because the old have the first chance, and are originally stronger—but is not at all rare, and has prevailed among our own progenitors more recently than we usually suppose. In the churches of Sweden there used to be kept wooden clubs, some of which have been preserved to the present day. They were called "family clubs" and were used to end ceremonially the lives of those who had become aged or hopelessly ill.

As man climbed painfully up the ladder of civilization, this conflict took on the social aspect of the antagonism between population and standard of living. Always and everywhere the inhabitants of a region have tended to increase up to a point which not only threatened the marginal classes with starvation, but lowered the general level of material existence of the entire group. It was the realization of this truth that led Malthus, the "gloomy parson", to proclaim the impossibility of any perfected state of human society and to condemn mankind to a perpetual future of misery, the only choice being between two evils, the greater misery of the "Positive checks" and the lesser misery of the "Preventive checks."

In the case of the individual family, this ineluctable conflict, before the coming of birth control and in the classes where birth control is not yet established, takes the aspect of a choice between restricted enjoyment of sex life in marriage and a superabundant number of children. In those classes where birth control has made the number of children a matter of deliberate choice and planning the alternative is the more specific one of size of family versus welfare of family. The problem is one in division. Family income over number of members equals what? Here simple hunger becomes expanded into the desire for material wellbeing, and its opponent is not the elemental sex urge, but a well-defined desire for children. But the antithesis still remains a choice between two contradictory goods. The sharp decline of the birth rate in recent decades indicates a well-defined tendency to decide in favor of welfare.

On the international plane this fundamental antagonism underlies all the struggle for colonies, the competition for markets, the rivalry in naval construction, the stimulus to population growth in the very face of the evil consequences of overpopulation, all the seething hostilities that eventually break forth in armed conflict.

The outstanding illustration of this principle at the present moment is being furnished by Japan. For centuries previous to its "opening up" to Western civilization, Japan, by methods best known to itself, had preserved a nearly stationary population and had maintained a relatively prosperous and tranquil existence. Then, under the impact of "modern culture", it proceeded to double its population in about fifty years, and is still adding 700,000 or 800,000 a year. The density of population in Japan proper is 404 persons to the square mile, and since less than twenty per cent of the land is being tilled, or probably ever can be tilled, the actual congestion is terrific. Until some means are applied for producing a drastic check in the rate of increase, Japan is forced to choose between the alternative of a declining standard of living and vigorous aggressive action externally.

III

Other aspects of the great antithesis are connected with traditional beliefs, aspirations, and philosophical dogmas that have become thoroughly ingrained in the cultural soul of Western peoples. The Eighteenth Century bequeathed us a heterogeneous lot of aphorisms, representing ideas which had a definite utility at the time they were expounded, but which have no foundation in enduring verity—illustrating the principle, not at all in accord with the Sunday School books, that things which are not true may often be useful, unless you beg the question by defining truth as that which serves a purpose. Foremost among these are Liberty, Equality, and Freedom. So popular were they in their day and so convincing, that the political and social structure of the United States was built upon them as upon the bedrock of reality. Yet taken together, they are thoroughly incongruous and incompatible. The whole history of democracy is a record of the attempt to harmonize Liberty and Equality, and we are just now beginning to realize that it can't be done.

Western Europe and the United States have tended to lean heavily toward liberty, with the result that there have developed those monstrous inequalities which have made modern society so topheavy that it threatens to go down in complete collapse, dragging liberty and all other civilized values with it. Russia, on the other hand, chose the pathway that stressed equality, and has been in process of learning how heavy is the price that must be paid in the loss of liberty. Apparently, however, Russia is at the same time developing the technic of compromise and producing a young generation that lays less store on either equality or liberty in their old, individualistic conception.

The reason for this impasse is that there is no innate, or natural, equality among human beings. All men are most emphatically not born equal, any more than they are born free. It did not need modern intelligence tests to demonstrate this, although the newer psychologies have given us further insight into the varieties of human equipment. The inequalities of men are physical, intellectual, and emotional. These are facts of nature, and we have as yet found no way to counteract them. Consequently,the only kind of equality that can be even hoped for in society is a formal, artificial, enforced equality which provides every man with the same opportunity to fend for himself and to make the most out of his native endowment. But if it is attempted to secure this goal under conditions of complete liberty it immediately happens that genuine equality of enjoyment, self-direction, and happiness fades into thin air and becomes merely pious aspiration. For men are not only unequal in ability but also in rapacity, shrewdness, ruthlessness, and guile. Under conditions of liberty there takes place a quick and spontaneous sifting whereby those who have certain qualities, not by any means all admirable, rise to positions of power and affluence, while others, perhaps far superior in social virtues and personal graces, are ground down to positions of ignominy and destitution. In fact, the very words "artificial" and "enforced" used in describing the only kind of possible equality indicate the inherent conflict with liberty. The only kind of equality that is possible is a socially guaranteed equality, and this can be secured only at the expense of liberty. It is closely accurate to say that factual equality must exist in inverse ratio to liberty.

This factual equality, in turn, brings its own dilemma. For it is incompatible with another axiomatic human desideratum, tranquillity. No amount of artificial reinforcement can offset the natural inequalities of human individuals. In spite of all restraints, the abler individual will reap certain rewards of achievement and satisfaction impossible to the less favored. But the latter, encouraged by the shibboleths of equality, will always be striving for the unobtainable, trying to prove, as the Irishman said, that "one man is as good as another, and far better," and reacting to their failure to reach their goal with envy, bitterness, and perhaps active turbulence. There can be no doubt that a large measure of the social disorganization and turmoil that characterize contemporary American life can be traced to the quixotic attempt to maintain the conditions of abstract equality among a population composed of the most heterogeneous elements, differing in both degrees and qualities of innate ability. So long as men are born as they are, the only really tranquil society is one in which a long-established caste system has graduated social status in close correspondence with inherited ability, or at least with routine aspiration, and where every individual is content to remain in the station in which his antecedents have placed him, whether his complaisance be due to lack of ability for anything higher or to absence of suggestion, from within or without, that a superior position might be open to him. Such a situation prevails in any thoroughly feudalistic society, such as England in the Middle Ages. Social relationships are governed by status, and it occurs to no one seriously to question them. When the idea of contract, which prevails in modern society, supervenes to throw the responsibility for social and economic station upon each individual, encouraging each to hope for the maximum, it inevitably creates bitterness and discontent among those who are in no measure fitted to force their way to the top. England up to the time of the World War still retained some of the aspects of the earlier type of social organization.

But such a situation is obviously incompatible with the principles of democracy, and once more a conflict arises. Speaking of democracy, an even more baffling antithesis is that between democracy and efficiency. Here are two of the cherished dogmas of the modern American philosophy, and yet, whether in the field of economics or politics, their incongruity has been so conclusively demonstrated that no discussion of the point seems necessary. Yet we cling pathetically to both of them in the vain hope that some sort of harness may be devised that will coerce them into pulling effectively in a given direction.

Another ill-assorted pair of philosophic objectives are Peace and Freedom. As already stated, we have craved freedom ever since the dawn of the modern era. Now, more perhaps than ever before, the whole world is yearning and striving for peace. The enthusiastic hope with which both are pursued is illustrated in the name of that highly esteemed organization, the "Women's International League for Peace and Freedom." But how, in the name of all that is logical and realistic, can you have both peace and freedom? As already pointed out, the fallacy of that aspiration became crystal clear at the time of our entry into the World War. We were faced with a situation that left us in no doubt that the only means to freedom was the abandonment of peace. And conditions have not changed, nor will they change until there have been some profound alterations in human nature. The predatory spirit among nations is just as rampant and just as menacing to-day as it was in 1914 or 1917. And as long as the more virulent representatives of this spirit enjoy freedom the peace of the rest of the world will be in hazard.

This is the nemesis of all peace movements, as every objective student of the subject knows. All the talk of disarmament, of offensive and defensive wars, of the aggressor and the resister, cannot eliminate the danger that some nation, on whatever pretext may be most convenient, will start on the warpath, and that then the only hope for freedom on the part of a people that stands in its way will lie in the abandonment of peace. At the recent Anti-War Congress in New York, Henri Barbusse, the great French pacifist, stood on the platform—oddly enough, flanked on each side by two or three men in military uniforms—and spoke against war, while the audience roared itself hoarse with enthusiastic approval. But if, just at the moment when the throng was leaving the hall, the hum of motors had been heard and a fleet of airplanes from some suddenly hostile country had appeared over the city ready to annihilate it with gas bombs, how many of that crowd would not have been glad that the United States was fully equipped with pursuit planes and would not have greeted the men who manned them and those who aimed the anti-aircraft guns as heroes when the danger was over? This is not to belittle the objective of world peace or to decry all honest and intelligent efforts to secure it. We need everything of that sort that we can have. Strength to the arm of every sincere and level-headed pacifist! But it does emphasize how frightfully complex is the problem and how appallingly real is the antagonism between peace and freedom. It suggests the conclusion that the only possible road to world peace is through limitation of freedom enforced by world agencies on a world-wide basis. At any rate, a pious obliviousness to realities will not promote the end that all rational men seek.

IV

Finally, perhaps the most immediately menacing and baffling of all dilemmas at the present moment are those in the economic field. These are partly due to inconsistencies in the economic structure itself, and partly to contradictions between some characteristic phases of the economic system and certain philosophic dogmas that are supposed to underlie, to direct, and to justify it. Foremost in the former group is the dominating struggle for competitive profits in an economic organization which, by its very nature, makes unlimited monetary profits mathematically impossible. This inconsistency has been so thoroughly expounded in recent years that the profit-motive is quite generally recognized as the gnawing cancer in the whole body politic, and innumerable able thinkers are working on the problem of its eradication.

A concrete case of a serious economic dilemma was described a few months ago by Professor G. F. Warren, who is now having a prominent part in the effort to solve it. "The price level must be raised to the debt level, or the debt level must be lowered to the price level. This is a matter of grim reality that cannot be cured by psychology, confidence, or Government lending. We must choose between deflation and reflation. No country likes to change its monetary system, nor does any country like to go through wholesale bankruptcies and continue to have millions of unemployed. Our choice is not between two desirable things. (Or between a desirable and an undesirable thing.—H.P.F.) It is between two undesirable things." (Printers' Ink, October 19, 1933.) The Administration obviously chose the way of reflation, though, judging by external appearances, even an emancipated Administration was not prepared to go the whole way and adopt the good old-fashioned method of the printing press, but as a lesser evil attempted to attain the same result by doing necromantic things with the price of gold.

Of a similar nature is the clash of interests between producer and consumer, and the impossibility of satisfying both at the same time. In the first decade of this century the menace to prosperity was seen in the "high cost of living." To-day it is in low prices. As a consequence we have the ironic situation that while President Roosevelt is marshalling the full force of his administration in a campaign to raise prices, Mrs. Roosevelt finds it expedient to warn the consumers that they must learn to protect themselves against too high prices or too sudden rises.

If the average American were asked whether he thought it was a good thing for his country to have a high wage scale among its working people he would undoubtedly give an affirmative answer. If, a day or so later, he were asked whether he thought it desirable to have low costs of production in industry, his reply would be an emphatic "Yes!" But the two are diametrically opposed to each other, for wages are an important element in the cost of production. Our politico-economic history for the past two generations has been largely a blind and unguided attempt to attain these two incompatible goods.

In the philosophic group the outstanding doctrines which gum up the wheels of progress and put a heavy drag on the instruments of prosperity are the familiar shibboleths of laissez faire and individualism. It will be apparent at a glance that these are closely allied to the principles of equality, liberty, and freedom, and that their pernicious influence in the economic realm is similar to that of the more generalized shibboleths in the social sphere. Some day the history of laissez faire will be written, and it will then appear that it has had a more maleficent influence on human destiny than perhaps any other doctrine devised by the human brain. It is not difficult to understand that one source of its baneful power is in the very utility which it possessed when first introduced. It was because it served as such an effective instrument for human advancement in one stage of cultural evolution that it acquired an almost axiomatic character, and continued to occupy a central position in the philosophic arsenal of the Western world long after conditions had so completely altered as to make it no longer an asset but a menace and a source of unmeasured disaster.

The same is true of individualism. Virtually the equivalent of personal liberty, this ideal has maintained a stranglehold on social thought sufficient to contribute decisively to world collapse, and at the present time is probably the most powerful agency in the prevention of really constructive and workable programs of recovery and permanent stabilization of the economic life and restoration of prosperity. The basic steps essential to the establishment of an economic system in harmony with the development of material technology and the general structure of modern society and at the same time consistent with the tenets of abstract social justice and human welfare are now quite well understood by the impartial and emancipated students of the problem. But every one of these measures comes up more or less squarely against the intrenched principle of individualism. A modern, enduring, tangible good is pitted directly against an ancient, tenderly cherished, philosophical good. Society must choose—there is no escape. To postpone the decision will not obviate the necessity. It will only aggravate the evils and make the final action more difficult. As in all such cases, the pathway of progress is blocked by our tendency to see much more clearly the defects and inconveniences of that which is new and different than of that which is familiar. Our chronic inability to grasp the nature of the great antithesis causes us to judge a novel program as a thing apart, in the abstract, rather than in its relation to that which it is intended to supplant. If we discern unattractive features in it we discard it without stopping to ask whether the present situation is not even more objectionable. Professor Warren recognizes the folly of this. "Merely raising the well-known objections to either procedure does not commend the other. The question is: 'Which is worse?' " But we are not in the habit of raising this question.

And so we hang back. The irresistible logic of events is moving us inevitably into some highly socialized form of community organization and life. But we—instead of recognizing the situation and devoting our energies to devising means to make the transition smooth, orderly, and constructive, we face backward, dig in our toes, and allow ourselves to be dragged along like a stubborn bull-pup at the end of a leash.

The real question is, can humanity grow up quickly enough to save itself from destruction? We are still in the stage of adolesence or childhood—which you prefer depends on the degree of your optimism. We still insist on eating our cake and having it too. We want to drive the family automobile with the same abandon that we use with a nursery toy. We continue to pretend that we are in fairyland while we walk the streets of the city.

It is a race between the growth of the human spirit to maturity of outlook and the internal forces of social disintegration. The issue lies in the lap of the gods.

2

PROFITS V. PROSPERITY

Written in 1932

"Fourteen Billion Dollars Lost in Stocks in Day." Thus the newspapers described the events of October 29, 1929. And tens of thousands of persons, the country over, were painfully convinced that it was true. Since then the loss has continued until now it amounts to over fifty-seven billions on the New York Stock Exchange List alone. And the American people as a whole feels poorer than it has felt for years.

But what, in reality, has been lost? Not money—there was scarcely half as much money in the country as the loss on that one day. In fact, there is considerably more money in the country now than there was on the day mentioned.

Not capital. Capital is correctly defined as material goods used in the production of wealth. There are just as many factories, machines, department stores, steamships, locomotives and cars and miles of railroad today as there were in 1929.

Not utility. These instruments of production are just as capable of turning out goods as they were two years ago.

Not stocks and bonds. All of these beautifully printed

and impressively signed sheets of paper would, if placed end to end, extend just as many times round the world as before the slump.

What has been lost is value—money value, fictitious value. And it has been lost just because it was fictitious. What was lost was never there.

Our present sense of poverty is due to a pervasive and pernicious dual fallacy, the fallacy of computing wealth in terms of capital and evaluating capital in terms of money. Intrinsically—that is, viewed in the light of the purpose for which it exists—our capital is worth just as much as it ever was. What its money value is is of no consequence whatever. We are indeed poor today, but it is not because of a depreciation in capital, but because of a shrinkage in the true substance and measure of wealth—purchasing power. If the purchasing power of the country could be doubled overnight we should suddenly find ourselves a rich people once more. The value of capital would probably rise accordingly, but this would be an effect of our riches, not a cause or a measure of them.

The value of capital is not in itself, but in the goods that it is capable of producing. The value of the goods, in turn, is in the possibility of their being sold in the general market. And, finally, the possibility of their being sold is dependent on the aggregate purchasing power of the market. Discover the way to restore purchasing power and you have discovered the remedy for the existing depression. Find out how to maintain purchasing power and you have found out how to prevent depressions in the future.

Our whole confusion in this matter is a result and a manifestation of our inveterate habit, in which we have been trained for a century and a half, of thinking of ourselves as producers instead of consumers—one of the most remarkable instances of inverted logic on a large scale that mankind has ever displayed.

II

Closely related to the capital-wealth fallacy, and a part of the same topsy-turvy philosophy, is another widespread misconception, even more devastating in its consequences—the illusion that a nation may get indefinitely rich by saving and investing. This is a concrete expression of the prevalent assumption that what is good for the individual is necessarily good for society. The truth, on the contrary, is that there is a rather numerous group of social evils for which the obvious personal remedy is not only no social remedy at all but may actually aggravate the social situation. A simple and pertinent illustration of this truth is found in a period of unemployment like the present. When there are not enough jobs to go round, the natural solution for the individual is to improve his economic efficiency in the hope of increasing his chances of getting one of the jobs that exist. But this does not increase the number of jobs, and if he succeeds in securing one it simply means that some other worker loses his job. And if any large number of workers adopt this expedient, thereby materially increasing the productive effectiveness of the entire labor force, the result is to intensify the tendency to overproduction that is the basis of the whole trouble, and so to make the general unemployment that much worse.

The futility of attempting to solve such a situation by personally desirable methods may be illustrated by the offering of a concert that will attract twelve hundred persons in a hall that will seat one thousand. Obviously, the personal remedy for you and me is to go early. But that does not solve the social situation—two hundred persons will still have to stand. And the larger the number of individuals who adopt this personal solution, the worse will be the resulting confusion and the greater the total amount of time wasted. The only real solution is to hire a larger hall—or a poorer singer.

The realization of this distinction is what creates the difference between social work and social engineering. It is social engineering for which the urgent need exists today. Social remedies, based on a scientific understanding of the factors and forces involved, are the only means of bringing back good times.

The specific fallacy that national prosperity may be achieved by the same means as personal prosperity is of ancient origin. It was the central tenet in the doctrines of the school of economists known as the Mercantilists. Perhaps its best known expression is in the book by Thomas Mun, "England's Treasure by Foreign Trade." The basic idea was that a nation might get rich by selling more than it bought, and thereby piling up accumulations of the precious metals. It is exactly this idea that lies back of the familiar phrase, "a favorable balance of trade." The same idea is inherent in the notion that a nation which has been victorious in war may enrich itself by exacting money payments from the loser—a fallacy eloquently and brilliantly exposed by Sir Norman Angell in his epochal book, "The Great Illusion."

The understanding of this group of fallacies rests upon a clear comprehension of the nature of modern wealth, particularly capital, and of the business system that has been built up around it.

III

If at this point in our discussion it is necessary to put on the academic cap and gown and delve into economic theory, let the reader not be dismayed. The application to our present business predicament will shortly be clear.

The first key to modern business is co-ordination of factors. The typical productive enterprise of today is carried out by the combination of two or more out of a total of five basic factors. Four of these factors are very well known. They are land, labor, capital, and organization. The first two are indispensable: no production can be carried on without land and labor. A simple illustration is furnished by a child picking huckleberries and eating them. But only an infinitesimal proportion of actual production is carried on without capital. It is the enlarged importance of capital, and its domination of the entire economic field, that have caused the present to be known as the capitalistic era, and at the same time have unfortunately obscured the significance of one or two of the other factors.

In order that land, labor, and capital may be combined into an effective unit, some directive skill, initiative, and control are necessary to determine the relations of these factors to one another and to guide their operations. This element has come to be known as "organization," and it, too, is virtually indispensable, being present in a minor degree in even so simple an activity as the child picking berries.

Such an organized combination of land, labor, and capital is the characteristic productive unit of the modern economic system. More and more, all businesses of every sort are coming to be conducted on this basis, with each of the four factors clearly recognized and delineated, and each given its appropriate place in the general scheme. It is the dominance of this type of unit that gives the color to modern economic life and determines its trend. When all businesses are organized on this basis the modern system will have reached its perfect flower, and its characteristic tendencies will be exerting their full influence. Such a culmination is clearly previsioned in modern life, and the evil nature of some of its consequences is already distressingly plain.

Such a productive unit is clearly a definite whole, and as a whole it must belong to somebody. This brings us to the fifth factor, which is the second key to modern business—ownership. This fifth factor, although seldom mentioned in the ordinary discussions, is just as indispensable as either land or labor. It has been strangely misunderstood or ignored in the traditional and conventional teaching of economics. Every budding young economist prates glibly about land, labor, capital, and organization. Very few, if any, realize that ownership is an equally distinct and equally important factor in production. It is this lapse on the part of the technical economic advisers of modern society that contributes largely to the existing chaos.

The reasons for this lapse, to be sure, are not difficult to discover. In the early Nineteenth Century, when the new industrial order was beginning to take shape, and when the new science of Economics was being developed as its intellectual god-parent, the factors of production were not nearly so clearly differentiated as at present, and the factor of ownership, in particular, was so completely merged in one or another of the others as to be wholly obscured. The dominant element in production was the figure, so exalted in conventional economic analysis, of the entrepreneur. He was likely to combine in his own person the functions of landowner, capitalist, and organizer. He also owned the business. But his ownership of the business was so wholly taken for granted that it never occurred to him to distinguish it as a separate function, and the economists did not perceive the logical necessity of doing so.

But with the development of the modern type of business, particularly the joint-stock form of ownership, all this has changed. There are now five—rather than four —basic and distinct factors in production. Indeed, the segregation of ownership as a separate factor is just as characteristic of modern economic life and just as determinative of its traits as the expansion of capital. That such a factor exists, and that it is independently rewarded by society, may be illustrated by the case of a young American who has inherited a business from his grandfather. He himself has contributed no land, no labor, no capital, nor any organizing skill. He takes no part in the running of the business; the entire staff, including the manager, having come to him with the business. In an extreme case he may not even know what the business produces. He spends his whole time in Europe and comes no nearer to engaging in actual production than supporting the gambling establishments of Monte Carlo and the race tracks at Longchamps and Auteuil. But society recognizes his place in the scheme of things and compensates him with an income.

Now the characteristic feature of ownership in most Western societies is that it is vested in private persons, individuals or legal persons. Indeed, this is so characteristic that merely to mention it seems superfluous. But this is precisely one of those commonplaces which are so familiar that their significance is not comprehended and which must be visualized in order to understand the nature of everyday phenomena. Private ownership of businesses is not necessarily inherent in human nature, nor in society. They might be owned by groups, or by society itself.

The third key to the modern business system is profit. This is unquestionably the dominating motive in contemporary economic life. Our whole industrial and commercial organization is geared up to the idea of profits. Profits are the goal of every business enterprise, the rosy dream of every young go-getter who clasps in his moistly eager hand the crisp certificate from business college or correspondence school. Profits of fifty or one hundred per cent are the ear-marks of successful stock investments or market manipulations. Everywhere is the tacit assumption that profits may be permanent, universal, unlimited in volume.

A remarkable statement of this doctrine was furnished by John J. Raskob in an interview in the "Ladies' Home Journal" for August, 1929, entitled "Everybody Ought To Be Rich." After dilating upon the wealth-producing qualities of common stocks and the desirability of borrowing in order to consume and to invest, the author concludes with the statement, "The way to wealth is to get into the profit end of wealth production in this country." That such a statement could be written only three or four months before the great crash demonstrates the complete lack of grasp of fundamentals on the part of some of the business leaders of the country.

There is no aspect of modern economic life so little understood, even by professionals and experts, as profits.

It is this failure to understand that accounts largely for the futility and confusion of the immediate situation.

Let us attempt to get a clear picture of the nature of profits, the reason for their existence, the possibilities of their expansion, and the limitations within which they develop.

IV

Under a system of private ownership of property, including businesses themselves, every factor in production must be compensated by society; otherwise it will not be supplied. The peculiar compensation of each of the four familiar factors has long been recognized, and elaborately expounded, by economists. Each has its name. The reward of land is rent, that of capital is interest, that of labor is wages, and that of organization—well, we are forced to confess that on this point the economists are far from unanimous and far from clear. They talk vaguely of salaries and of profits and of residual claims. This uncertainty, however, is easily traceable to their failure to recognize ownership as a separate factor, with profit as its reward. As a name for the reward of organization, in the absence of a better word, we may adopt the term "salaries."

Profit, then, properly defined is the reward that society pays to individuals for the ownership of businesses, and of nothing else—not of capital, nor of land, nor of labor.

But why should individuals be rewarded merely for ownership?

From Socialist ramparts, far and near, resounds the echo, Why?

This, however, does not settle the problem. Certainly

a practice so widespread, so nearly universal, must have an explanation, if not a justification.

In the first place, under the existing system, businesses must be owned by someone; and nobody would bother to own them if there were not some reward. There is, however, in addition one genuine service that the owner renders—he does assume the basic risk of the business as such. The landlord, the laborer, the capitalist, the manager are all supposed to be guaranteed their returns—a supposition, alas! all too often contrary to fact. But in theory there is a contract between them and the owner which assures them of their income. To be sure, the security of this contract depends on the stability of the business; and everyone participating in the business runs some chance of loss. It must also be recognized that, in spite of recurring industrial depressions, the risks of ownership are largely reduced by the stabilization of industrial processes and the possible wide diversification of holdings. If such a depression represents risk, surely the other elements of production bear their share of it. But even so, the risk of the owner stands in a class by itself.

In the last analysis, however, it must be admitted that the owner gets his return because he *can* get it, and our concern at present is not so much to inquire why he should get it as how he can get it, and how much he can get, and for how long.

The owner of the business can get a profit because he owns the product. The total output of a productive unit belongs to the owner of that unit, and to him alone.

This is another feature of our modern mores and economic law which is universally taken for granted, and of which, just because it is taken for granted, the significance is almost completely obscured. There is a vast amount of muddy thinking on the subject. We hear frequent repetition of such phrases as "labor's share of the product." Now only in a figurative and moralistic sense has labor any share in the product. Never, at any time, does any part of the product actually belong to labor. *Out* of the product labor receives its compensation. But this is not because of any ownership of the product, but because labor's contract with the owner calls for compensation, and the owner has nowhere else to get it from than the product.

The same thing is true of the other three factors in production. Neither the landlord, the capitalist, nor the manager *as such* ever owns one iota of the product. That prerogative inures to the owner alone.

If the owner can meet all his fixed obligations for land, labor, capital, and management, and other charges on the business such as the cost of raw materials, advertising, insurance, bribing of legislatures, etc., and have anything left, he has a chance of a profit. All of these expenses, of every kind, must first be paid out of the product.

Of course, in real life all these transactions are carried on in terms of money. Particularly, the product does not take on its full significance until it is transmuted into money. This means that it must be sold. The situation may, therefore, be expressed thus: The owner's only chance of profit consists in selling the product for more than it has cost to produce it. Any excess in the selling price over the cost of production represents clear profit. The whole crux of this inquiry then is, How, and to what extent, can owners of businesses sell their goods above the cost of production? The whole future of the capitalistic system hinges upon the correct answer to this question. It is a matter of common observation that an individual owner may do so. The fallacy alluded to lies in the assumption that *all* owners may do so. To demonstrate that it is an impossibility necessitates an inquiry into the nature of the market, the sources and extent of purchasing power.

V

For this purpose let us imagine the present tendencies of economic evolution carried to their full efflorescence. Let us also exclude all consideration of foreign markets, which would not affect the basic principles but would complicate the exposition. Let us imagine, then, a perfectly capitalized, self-contained society.

In such a society every productive activity of every sort, large and small, would be organized on a strict business or accounting basis. In every business each contributing factor would be distinctly identified and specifically rewarded. No person would be engaging in any productive task except as a landlord, a laborer, a capitalist, a manager, or an owner. If any individual combined two or more of these functions in his own person his total income would be properly assigned accordingly. All income, therefore, would consist of rent, wages, interest, salaries, and profits. All but the last would be fixed in amount by contract with the owners. The owners—the sole participators who work on a contingent basis—would be rewarded by the residual item of profits.

These profits would depend upon the total purchasing power of the society. This, in turn, would be equivalent to the total income of the society apart from profits, which finally would consist of two main categories. First, the aggregate of rent, wages, interest, and salaries paid by all the businesses. Second, the total amount of a miscellaneous item, withdrawn from previous products, which may be called "owner's advances," and which includes the cost of all materials, insurance, advertising, etc. But the total of these two categories is also precisely the total cost of production of the aggregate product. In such a society, accordingly, the total purchasing power of the market is exactly equivalent to the total cost of production. How, then, can the product be sold for more than the cost of production? Where is the extra purchasing power to come from? The answer is flatly, It cannot be sold for more than the cost of production. There is no surplus purchasing power.

How, then, can there be any profits?

In such a situation there is just one possible way of achieving profits—a *part* of the product may be sold for an amount equal to the *total* cost of production. The remaining portion of the product may be made a source of profit. But how, and to what extent? That is the nub of the whole problem.

Suppose that this process has been carried out. Let us say that four-fifths of the product has been sold for an amount equal to the total cost of production, leaving the owners in possession of the remaining fifth. Is this surplus product profit, or can it be turned into profit? In one sense it is profit. The owners have a lot of goods on their hands that are exclusively theirs, which have cost them nothing. The shoe manufacturer has twenty thousand pairs of shoes, the radio manufacturer three thousand radios, and the farmer five hundred head of cattle. No owner need lack for goods of his own production. But this would be a very dreary and disillusioning conception of profits.

There is just one other possibility. The owners may trade—or in a money economy, sell—their goods to one another. The final problem as to the ultimate possibilities of profits depends upon the extent to which this can and will be done and what returns in human satisfaction it yields if it is done.

To aid in the analysis of this problem let us imagine first of all a society in which the concentration of ownership has been carried to its extreme culmination. There is just one owner—all the businesses belong to him. He has sold four-fifths of the product to the rest of his fellow-citizens, for an amount equal to the total cost of production and the total income of the society, and he now possesses the remaining one-fifth. What can he do with it? Obviously, he cannot sell it—nobody has any money to buy it with. There is just one thing he can do with it—*he can consume it.*

Such a man would certainly be the wealthiest person in his society. He could live in a degree of luxury unimaginable to the ordinary citizen. He could so manipulate the production of society as to leave a minimum surplus of the common staples that he did not wish and a maximum surplus of those refined products that brought him pleasure. But his wealth would not be infinite. Only those goods would constitute wealth which he could actually use for his own gratification. All the rest of his surplus product would be absolutely meaningless. In brief, his profits would be limited by his capacities for personal enjoyment of material things.

Now suppose that, instead of one owner, there were two, each owning residually one-tenth of the total product. They would naturally exchange goods with each other, and each might enjoy all the material delights that his heart could wish. But above that, the excess goods would be totally without significance, for there would still be nobody to buy them. The profit of each would be limited by his personal capacity to enjoy. So if there were ten owners, or a thousand, or ten thousand, the situation would remain the same. So long as the surplus profit remaining above the cost of production were sufficient to give each all the material supplies he craved, the profit of each would be equivalent to his capacity to consume. It might be less, but it could never be more.

There thus emerges what appears to be a general law: In a fully capitalized society true profits must always be limited by the owners' capacity to consume.

VI

Now, how does all this link up with the actual facts of life? To what extent are these hypothetical conditions realized in the contemporary economic situation? Is the foregoing generalization applicable to the living owners of today and their profits?

There are obviously some important divergencies. In the first place, the entire productive activity of a modern society is by no means completely reduced to an exact accounting basis. The various factors of production are hard to identify, and the "tagging" of the various items of income is difficult to accomplish. It is particularly hard to differentiate profits from other kinds of income. In the second place, ownership is not confined to a single group of persons who participate in production simply as owners and nothing else. Nor is the actual ownership so highly concentrated as the illustration assumes. It is very widely dispersed. There are millions of petty stockholders who own only a few shares apiece, but who are, nevertheless, to be included in the total factor of ownership.

Nevertheless, there is a very significant resemblance in a modern society to the situation outlined. While there are enormous numbers of small owners, especially in agriculture, there is at the same time a relatively small group of persons whose ownings make up a very considerable portion of the whole; so much so that highly concentrated ownership is really a feature of modern life. As a hint, though not an exact expression, of this situation, may be cited the estimate that in the United States one ten-thousandth of those who realize income get over one-fiftieth of the income. Also while all production is not yet reduced to the standard economic pattern, yet there is a powerful tendency in that direction; and a very large proportion of the total activity is carried on through large concerns organized in that way. And this is what is really important in a discussion of this sort, which concerns itself with the characteristics and manifest destiny of an economic system organized on a complete profit basis.

The central fact is that a very large proportion of the product, on completion, belongs to a very small group of exceedingly wealthy persons, who dominate the situation. Their position is fundamentally similar to that of the small group of owners assumed in our hypothetical illustration. They are the ultimate holders of enormous amounts of goods which are left after the public has consumed as much of the product as it will at prices sufficiently high to leave a "margin of profit." Their problem is what to do with these goods, and it is the difficulty—indeed, the impossibility—of finding an answer to this problem satisfactory to them that lies at the very root of many of our modern economic evils, including such depressions as the present.

Owners such as these can have, practically speaking, all the consumption goods they wish. If the theory, so prominent in economic analyses, that human wants are unlimited, were true, they would have little fault to find, and society would suffer only from the spectacle of their hyperluxurious living. But the theory is not true. Persons of extreme wealth practically never want to spend all their income on personal consumption. A very large portion of it they wish to save and invest. John Jacob Astor is reported to have said, "I can do nothing with my income but buy more land, build more houses, and lend money on mortgages." But before the excess goods can be invested they must be sold and turned into money. And there is no way of selling them. For the whole purchasing power of the community has been expended in returning to the owners the entire cost of production in exchange for a portion of the product. Naturally, the larger the amount of product held out for profit the greater is the difficulty of turning it into profit. This is the inevitable dilemma of all owners, the nemesis of the profit system.

Any person may demonstrate to himself the falsity of the assumption that human wants are unlimited, with respect to the goods that exist at any given time, by imagining himself possessed of unlimited purchasing power, and then asking himself how many of each particular item he would buy in a year—how many pounds of beefsteak, pairs of shoes, toothbrushes, opera tickets, Rolls Royce cars, private yachts, all the items in a Sears,

Roebuck catalogue. He will discover that his desires for every particular class of goods and, therefore, for all classes of goods, are strictly limited. And if the desires of each individual are limited, the aggregate desires of society is limited. With purchasing power highly concentrated in a relatively small group, as it is in modern society, the effective limitation on the demand for goods becomes greatly increased beyond what it would be if purchasing power were evenly divided.

There is, to be sure, one seeming avenue of escape, which is readily enough perceived by any intelligent owner, and eagerly seized upon by owners as a class. This is to manipulate production in such a way that a large part of the product, instead of appearing in the form of consumable goods, will be capital in the true sense of the word, that is, goods designed for use in the production of more goods. It is theoretically possible for owners as a class to arrange things so that the surplus product left after they have gratified their consumption wants shall all be in the form of capital and shall promptly be set to work producing more goods.

Unfortunately, this process is not permanent in character, but is inherently self-limiting and self-destructive. For the ultimate purpose and justification of all production is the creation of consumption goods; and the final requirement of a healthy state of production is that all these goods shall be consumed. The more the productive plant is enlarged, the greater is the total volume of the product, and the larger the proportion remaining unsalable after the purchasing power of the market has been exhausted. The sole motive for investment is the hope of selling the product at a profit. The multiplication of the product on a system essentially unstable simply aggravates the evil. The whole idea of maintaining prosperity by a constant increase of invested wealth is excellently characterized by the classic example of the village that undertook to support itself by taking in one another's washing.

This is particularly true because the big owner is usually also a capitalist. His income includes interest as well as profit. By increasing his capital he augments also his interest, thereby enabling him to satisfy his consumer wants, and leave a still larger portion of his surplus product to be disposed of. Indeed, it would doubtless be economically preferable if the large owners spent their entire incomes in the most fantastic extravagances of consumption, though the social repercussions might be bad enough to more than offset the gain.

Not only owners, but income receivers of every sort who can squeeze out a little surplus above their consumptive expenditures, are continually yielding to the temptation to spend this surplus for production goods, land or capital, that is, to invest it. In "good times" this seems to be a desirable and natural thing to do. For a while things continue to run along very smoothly. Owners invest a large part of their profit receipts in new production plant, and others invest what they can. This increases the demand for goods of various sorts, especially raw materials, and also for labor, land and managerial skill. This creates a temporary impression of prosperity, and owners are encouraged to put still more of their income to productive uses. So it goes on. But all the time the volume of surplus product, actual and potential, is rolling up, and eventually, usually rather suddenly, owners wake up to the fact that their businesses have turned out more goods than can possibly be "sold at a profit," and are busily engaged in multiplying the surplus. Panic-stricken, they issue orders to curtail production, shut down plants, lay off men, cancel orders—and behold! a depression.

The key to the whole situation is in the nature of profits and the system of ownership. It needs no argument to show that the more widely ownership is distributed, and the greater the number of persons among whom the surplus product is divided, the greater is the chance of owners exchanging their surplus goods with one another, and eventually disposing of them all without exceeding the consumptive desires of any. If ownership was perfectly evenly divided, and the product owned on an exact per capita basis, there would be no excess product at all—unless the society were so mad that it kept on working feverishly because it had nothing else to do—but then, there would be no profits either. For when everybody owns just as much as you do, you cannot make anything out of your ownership.

And so it appears that the generalization stated above is not only true and applicable to existing conditions, but is actually operating in our midst. In the long run, and for society in general, profits are, and must be, limited to the owners' capacities for personal consumption.

That a depression like the present is fundamentally a matter of ownership and profits is shown by the fact that it manifests itself primarily in a slump in dividends and in the value of stocks. For stocks are simply certificates of part-ownership of businesses; and dividends, in the strict sense, are distributed profits. There is a vast amount of popular confusion on this subject, which adds to the difficulty of grappling practically with the defects of our economic system. This is due partly to a careless use of the word "capital." The average man uses the term capital to include all his invested funds, whether represented by stocks, bonds, mortgages, or even deeds to real estate. Correctly defined, the returns on bonds and mortgages are interest; the returns on land are rent. A part of a dividend may also fall in these categories, if the company in question has spent part of its stock receipts for the actual purchase of land or capital instruments. But the true dividend is a payment on that part of the cost of a share which represents actual ownership in the business as a whole. It is, therefore, profit. Consequently, when profits fall off dividends are cut down or discontinued. And since the value of a stock is dependent entirely on its dividends, the price of stocks descends to the depths.

The whole situation is due to the fact that the multiplication of product has outrun the effective purchasing power of the market. The inflated stock values of 1929 rested on delirious hope, not on any actual purchasing power. That is why they were never real.

We have already in this country a productive plant capable, if continuously and efficiently operated, of turning out about four times the amount of goods that we now produce. What colossal folly to imagine that we can increase our wealth and promote our prosperity by increasing this plant!

A more even distribution of purchasing power has frequently been urged in the past on grounds of justice or mercy. It is time now to realize that, apart from all sentiment, it is essential to the maintenance of prosperity and the preservation of economic stability in the most realistic sense. A social system in which a small proportion of the population has income far in excess of its desires to spend on personal consumption, while the great majority has consumptive desires far in excess of its income, is economically unsound from the foundations up.

VII

At this point the question naturally arises, if all this is true, how is it that the profit system has succeeded in maintaining itself and dominating society for so long?

The answer to this question is manifold. In the first place, it has not been for long. Compared with the whole span of human existence, the dominion of the profit system is but an instant of time. Nor, indeed, has it been eminently successful.

In the second place, the decades during which the rule of profits has forged to the front have been really only a transition period. The organization of society on a profit basis is still far from complete. A great deal can happen in a transition period that is quite different from —often diametrically opposite to—that which will prevail when the transition is complete. The process of "modernizing" industry has been of sufficient scope to maintain genuine, but ephemeral, conditions of prosperity over an extended period. But the basis of such prosperity is in the expansion, not in the nature of modern industry itself.

Again, there has always been a foreign market to affect the situation. Until recent years, this foreign market has been composed quite largely of countries which were not highly developed industrially and were not themselves organized on a profit basis. They have contributed to the realization of profits in the more advanced nations. The general spread of modernization and the profit motive over the world is undoubtedly one of the explanations of the worldwide character of the present depression.

Then again, during this period there have not only been profits—there have also been losses. And every loss makes possible a profit. Every time goods are sold for less than the cost of production it releases that much money to buy other goods at more than the cost of production. This is why some individuals can do what all individuals cannot do. While it would doubtless be a gross exaggeration to say that during the past hundred years the losses in industrial society have equalled the profits, yet they must have offset them to a very considerable degree. The losses of a depression like the present eat up the profits of a long antecedent period.

But probably most important of all is the fact that production has not been carried out on a strict accounting basis. Particularly, many values have entered into the total income of society which have not been credited to any particular account. Foremost in this category are various irreplaceable natural resources, both of an agricultural and mining character. The appropriation and depletion of the farm and forest lands in this country, the withdrawal of iron, coal, gas, and oil, not to mention a host of other substances, have released a sufficient value for which no accounting is made to provide for a stupendous total of apparent but spurious profits. Society as a whole has lost as much as it has gained in these directions.

And so in the end our inquiry into the nature of profits leads us to the conclusion that the possibility of profits increases in direct proportion with the increase in the number of owners. But as the recipients of profits increase, the per capita profits diminish until they cease to be a significant motive. Thus we arrive at the seeming paradox, which, nevertheless, contains the vital principle of the matter: General profits are possible only when they are so widely dispersed that there cease to be any profits at all. A social system that allows itself to be dominated by the profit motive is doomed to recurrent calamity and eventual catastrophe.

3

POPULATION V. PEACE

Written in 1925

WE MUST SUPPOSE that there are some persons who cherish war for its own sake, who discern in the very act of war the springs of certain cultural or moral values quite apart from the recognized objectives of war or the tangible rewards of victory. But these can hardly be numerous enough, at least in a democratic nation where the will of the people determines group action, deliberately to plunge their country into war simply for the sake of the discipline of fighting. Those who are laboring for a war-less world can afford to devote a very limited portion of their energies to this obstacle.

Much more serious is the idea that war is due to a natural and ineradicable characteristic of human beings, which it is impossible to eliminate and useless to try to suppress or control. The social psychologists make much of the instinct of pugnacity, ranking it with hunger and love as an elemental source of human conduct. But it is a shallow and rudimentary philosophy which seeks to explain the doings of men on the basis of a catalogue and classification of instincts. So in the case of war, in whatever proportions the motives be distributed between instinct and reason, there must always be a positive objective.

Men fight because there is something to be gained by fighting. In the thing or things for which they fight is to be found the ultimate cause of war, and only as this cause can be mastered is there any hope of controlling war. Attempts to "cure" war by any other means than by eradicating the cause are as futile as putting a piece of pink court plaster over a festering sore. The effect may be to improve temporarily the superficial aspect; but the final result is to make things worse.

Is there, then, any one cause of war? If we push our inquiry beneath the surface of the multitudinous and apparent causes of specific wars, there emerges an almost universal and fundamental objective in war,—land.

Men fight, and always have fought, for land. Sometimes the ultimate objective is removed one stage and the actual immediate struggle is for the products of land. But the meaning is the same. Land is desired only for its products, and the surest way to get the products is to get the land. As long as men desire land keenly enough to pay the price of the losses of war, there will be war. The only way to eliminate war is either to keep the desire for land below the point at which the sacrifices of war are voluntarily accepted, or else to make it impossible to get land by war. It is in various aspects of man's hunger for land that his human nature and his animal nature draw close together, or rather appear, as they are, identical. With all his marvelous human qualities and achievements man is yet an animal, one of innumerable organic species struggling for existence upon the limited surface of a planet. It thus comes about that the basic law of all social science is the basic law of biology.

This basic law may be stated: All life is dependent upon the land, that is, upon the substances which make up the earth's surface. The demands made upon the land by organic species are of two kinds, demands for food and demands for standing room. The former of these is universally recognized. The latter is often lost sight of, particularly in the case of man, for the reason that man, the highest product of organic evolution, uses so small a proportion of his total land holdings for standing room (dwelling purposes, etc.) that it is easy to forget to count it. But as we go lower in the scale of evolution the significance of standing room becomes more obvious. In the vegetable kingdom the demands for standing room and for food are identical. Let us consider, briefly, man's demand for food. Since he is an animal, his food quest must correspond in general to that of the animal kingdom, and in particular to those animal species most like him. Obviously there can be no more life of a specific type than can be supported on the amount of food of a particular sort that nature furnishes. Man is no exception to this law.

If we put together the factors of the fixed quantities of natural substances, the necessity of adaptation to a given environment, and the inevitable overlapping demands of different species, it becomes clear that the possibilities of life for any given species are subject to drastic and inflexible limitations. The first law of nature is the law of a positive limit to the increase of each species, and therefore of all species.

But the fact of an immovable limit to increase does not in itself necessarily involve struggle. Unless there exists some impulse driving species to press upon this limit there need be no conflict. There may be only a restricted amount of room, but unless this room is overcrowded the fact is of no practical significance. Is there, then, any force inherent in animal life that tends to expand each species until it presses positively upon its limit? If there is such a force it is obviously to be found in the reproductive tendency. It is therefore necessary to examine the essential features of this tendency.

The tendency of an organic species to increase consists of two elements, the capacity to increase and the impulse to increase. The capacity to increase, practically speaking, seems to be a question of the fecundity of the females, since the males are always able to fertilize whatever number of ova the females are able to produce. The fecundity of natural species varies between very wide extremes; in general it is of a startling magnitude. Examples are familiar to every student of evolution. A large oyster may lay sixty million eggs in a year; the average American yield is about sixteen million. The possibilities of increase involved in such fecundity are staggering. Starting with a single pair and breeding at the average American rate, the oysters of the fifth generation,—the great-great-grandchildren of the original pair,—would form a mass eight times the size of the earth. Havelock Ellis cites one minute organism whose rate of reproduction is so great that, if it were not checked, in thirty days it would form a mass a million times larger than the sun. But not even a high fecundity is necessary to produce tremendous totals in a very short time, granting full survival to all the offspring produced. Reproduction is, literally, multiplication and when unchecked proceeds at a geometrical ratio. A species of animals each pair producing ten pairs a year, and each animal living ten years would increase from a single pair to over 700,000,000,000,000,000,000 pairs in twenty years. The Fulmar petrel lays but one egg a year, yet Darwin believed it to be one of the most numerous birds on earth. As far as the capacity to increase is concerned, it is safe to say that there is not an organic species in existence, man included, which could not cover the earth in an incredibly short time if there were no checks.

Turning to the factor of the impulse to increase, we find that it matches effectively the capacity. In the natural course of events the operation of this impulse results in the fertilization of the great proportion of the ova which the female produces, and in the consequent birth of offspring approximating the physiological capacity of the female.

Millions of times more life is produced each year than the world can support. As a result, existence in nature is a ruthless and incessant orgy of killing. The toll of death is levied mainly on the newborn. Infant mortality in nature falls short of totality by an infinitesimal fraction of one per cent.

This is the basis of the struggle for existence in nature which has so impressed every student of evolution. The result of this struggle is a balance of nature, whereby each species, very soon after it becomes a separate species, increases up to the maximum limit set by the provisions furnished by the soil and the competition of the other species for those provisions, and then comes to a dead halt. The law of nature is a *stationary population.*

The application of these fundamental truths and principles to man, and their bearing on the problem of war, are obvious enough. Man began his earthly career as a new species, or perhaps, as some students prefer to believe, two or more independent species. For this species, or for each of these species, there was a niche in nature. This niche could be appropriated only as a result of successful conflict with those who were already utilizing the supplies furnished by the land. If man had not been equipped to win out in this competition there never would have been a human species. But he was equipped with certain unique advantages, mainly of hand and brain, which enabled him, by painful and immeasurably slow stages, to force his way into the natural economy and increase his numbers, while at the same time improving his equipment, and thereby enlarging the niche itself.

Man alone, of all the old species, has hitherto succeeded in escaping the fundamental law of stationary population. He has been able not only to increase his numbers, but to increase them at an accelerating ratio. These facts encourage some humans to believe that this record of achievement may be projected into an indefinite future. They see no reason to fear that the increase of mankind must eventually bring up against any fixed and immovable barriers.

Just at the beginning of the nineteenth century Thomas R. Malthus, the first student to attract widespread attention to the biological basis of the population problem, was painting the prospect of human increase in colors so dark as to cause him to be ranked as one of the arch-pessimists of all time. There were then about six hundred and forty million people in the world. The doctrine of Malthus was taken to imply that no notable further increase of the species could take place without involving untold misery and calamity. Yet what actually happened was this: Within the next hundred years the population of the world increased to 1543 million, and at the same time the general level of comfort, especially in the western countries where the rate of growth was highest, rose to a point far above any ever attained before in human experience. After consuming 500,000 years or more in producing two-thirds of a billion individuals, mankind suddenly added nearly a billion more in one hundred years with no loss in general well-being.

These remarkable facts are interpreted in diametrically opposite ways by different types of mind. There are the pious ones who say: "*A bas* Malthus! God will provide as much food as there are mouths to eat it." They see in the increase in population of the last century and a quarter evidence of a Divine solicitude. To others, the fact that we have multiplied at this unprecedented rate for the past one hundred and twenty-five years,—for we are still keeping it up,—is the very reason why we cannot continue to do so. If impending calamity is not visible to the naked eye, it is easily discernible through the medium of a reasoning intelligence.

There are still others who believe that we can trust the human mind rather than God to maintain an increasing mastery over nature sufficient to provide in undiminished measure for the needs of the human body, however multiplied. They maintain, in brief, that if sufficient attention is devoted to the problem of production the problem of reproduction will take care of itself.

While this economic interpretation may, and does, explain the extraordinary happenings of the past hundred and twenty-five years, it does not offer any justification for the belief that such an increase in population and well-being can continue indefinitely. Although the real purpose and effect of our economic civilization is to enable more men to live on a given area without a loss, or even with a gain, in material well-being, its method consists in manipulating natural forces in such a way as to make them conduce to the support of human life in preference to any other form of life, and not in adding to the total volume of life that can be supported on the earth's surface.

It is exceedingly important to recognize that all the marvelous achievements of human civilization in its material aspects have consisted merely in substituting human life for other forms of life. Our economic arts have consisted mainly in finding the uses of various forms of life and progressively eliminating those that do not contribute to the increase and comfort of human life.

It should be clear enough that the phenomenal increase of population of the past one hundred and twenty-five years is traceable directly to a unique combination of the expedients of movement and economic culture represented by the discovery of America and the modern immigration movement on the one hand, and the Industrial and Commercial Revolutions on the other. These two factors, coming together, gave the human species an entirely new chance, and enabled it to more than double its numbers while raising its level of comfort to an unprecedented point. If there is hope that this combination of advantages may be duplicated in the future, then there is hope that the present rate of increase may be kept up for a corresponding period.

Each individual must decide this question for himself as best he can. But there are certain conditioning facts which seem to be positively established. The first is that the expedient of movement as a peaceful means of providing for human increase has almost completely run its course. The modern immigration movement is just a temporary flurry, representing the redistribution of population, with an attendant large increase, which naturally followed the discovery of America and certain other thinly populated lands. The passage of a numerically restrictive law by the United States should serve as a signal that the era of peaceful, permitted population movements has about come to a close. After a few decades more there will be no countries left who will willingly receive large contingents of population from foreign sources. They will be sufficiently put to it to provide for their own increase. Any further large transfers of population must necessarily be carried out by force, through the instrumentality of war, and at the cost of innumerable human lives.

The expedient of economic culture still holds out promise. No one would be so rash as to attempt to put a period to the possibilities of supporting more human life through a more efficient utilization of the supplies furnished by the land. But it is absolutely certain that no amount of economic progress can provide for an indefinite or unlimited increase of population. Some time there must come a stop. Furthermore, it is vain to hope that economic progress can suffice to maintain even the present rate of increase for more than a very limited time. If the population of the world were to increase at the rate that prevailed just before the War, at the end of ten thousand years the resulting number would be 221,840, 000,000, 000, 000,000,000, 000,000,000, 000,000-000,000,000,000. The significance of the factor of standing room is shown by the fact that, allowing one and one-half square feet of standing room per person, this population would require 60,570,000,000, 000, 000, 000,-

000,000,000,000,000 times more standing room than the earth affords. If this culmination appears too remote to cause present concern, we may bring the matter nearer home. If the population of the United States were to keep on growing as it was growing just before the War, by the end of this century,—a date that many people now living will survive to see,—we should have conditions of overcrowding upon our territory considerably worse than China has to-day, and soon after the middle of the next century we should have as many people as the entire present population of the globe.

Confronted with these facts the "man on the street" characteristically replies with a complacent shrug, "Oh, well! that will never happen." True enough,—it never will happen. But the question is, What is to keep it from happening, the rule of nature or the exercise of human devices?

It has been shown that, of the two human expedients upon which man has relied hitherto to escape a stationary population and maintain a steady increase without engaging in war all the time, one has virtually exhausted itself and offers practically no relief for the future, and the other can not possibly be relied upon to provide for an increase at the rate called for by the present customary combination of the desire for wealth and the desire to mate. This is particularly true because civilized man demands from the earth much more than food, and many of his economic activities involve taking from the land substances,—iron, gas, oil, copper, and so forth,—which are not, and can not be, replaced in usable form.

Briefly stated, then, man has never succeeded in freeing himself from his dependence upon the land. Land will still remain the primary and preeminent economic desideratum. The amount of land is permanently fixed, and the increase of mankind at prevailing rates is not only making demands upon the land which can not possibly be met for more than a very brief time to come, but also practically destroying the very qualities of the land itself. As long as these conditions prevail periodic wars seem inevitable. As long as human groups continue to increase without restraint upon a restricted area of land we may confidently expect them, in the final extremity, to fly at each other's throats for the possession of what land there is, finding a pretext in national honor or invaded rights if one is to be found, and if not getting along without a pretext.

There remains just one possible avenue of escape, through the utilization of an expedient even more distinctively human than the two which have hitherto been employed. This expedient consists of consciously and rationally regulating the increase of the group in accordance with the possibilities of maintaining life already developed. Let reproduction follow production by a good safe margin. Instead of expecting God to provide as much food as there are mouths to eat it, see to it that there are never more mouths than can be adequately and comfortably fed. Any group that succeeds in establishing this expedient among its peoples will have emancipated itself from the outstanding incentive to aggressive war. And such a group should certainly not be expected to share its benefits with other groups less intelligent, less self-controlled, less human.

4

LIBERTY V. SECURITY

Written in 1928

"Enforce it or repeal it."

How familiarly the sentiment rings in our ears! And how unerringly we jump to the conclusion that it is the liquor law to which it refers!

A stranger to the United States, unfamiliar with the present situation and its background, would infer from all the clamor that among all our multitude of laws the prohibition law stood out unique for the failure or inadequacy of its enforcement. The truth is, on the contrary, that the uniqueness of the prohibition law lies in the fact that it is about the only important law that any one expects to be enforced. At first glimpse this statement may seem fantastic—but let us see.

Law is one of the most ancient, as it is the most concrete and explicit, of social expedients. One of the earliest consequences of an emerging group consciousness was the selection of certain acts of the individual to be placed under that definite proscription of the community which is law. It was natural that the first of the acts so designated should be those involving the greatest social injury, and at the same time most likely to be committed; specifically, attacks upon life and upon property. From time immemorial, therefore, all societies have had some form of laws against murder and against theft, and a considerable part of the energies of all states has been devoted to the enforcement of these laws. One might be justified in expecting, accordingly, that after uncounted centuries of effort in this direction the most modern and "civilized" states should have virtually mastered this problem, and that certainly in the United States the laws against murder and theft would be almost perfectly enforced. What are the facts?

That we have not succeeded in eliminating murder in the United States is a matter of all too common knowledge. It is perhaps not so generally known that our efforts in this direction are becoming steadily less successful. In 1882 the homicide rate was about 3 per 100,000 of the general population. In 1900, according to the careful compilations of Dr. Frederick L. Hoffman, the rate in twenty-eight American cities stood at 5.1 per 100,000. Since then it has increased steadily until in 1924 it reached 10.3 per 100,000 having more than doubled in a quarter of a century.

Some consolation for this situation, possibly, might be found if we were improving our technique for dealing with those guilty of these crimes. Unfortunately just the reverse is true. According to the figures of the Chicago Tribune, in 1882 the number of executions amounted to 8.25 per cent of the murders committed, in 1890 it was 2.37 per cent, and in 1899, 2.1 per cent. What the rate is at present, it is difficult to say, the Chicago Tribune apparently having discontinued its statistics, and the official figures being notoriously lacking.

The Homicide Bureau of the District Attorney's office of New York in 1920 investigated six hundred and seventy-nine killings which were reported as possible homicides. The bureau presented evidence to Grand Juries in one hundred and thirty cases, and obtained seventy-eight indictments. The net result in convictions for first degree murder was just one.

Strange that we hear no one crying out for the repeal of the law against murder!

Our record in the matter of theft is similar, though not capable of quite such concise statement.

In both these respects the showing of the United States is humiliating when compared with that of foreign countries. Mr. Raymond B. Fosdick in his "Crime in America and the Police," has given us some illuminating contrasts. "London in 1916, with a population of seven millions and a quarter, had nine premeditated murders. Chicago, one-third the size of London, in the same period had 105, nearly twelve times London's total. In the year 1916, indeed—and it was not an exceptional year—Chicago with its 2,500,000 people had twenty more murders than the whole of England and Wales put together with their 38,000,000 people. New York City in 1916 had exactly six times the number of homicides (murder and manslaughter) that London had for the same year, and only ten less homicides than all of England and Wales. In 1917 New York had six times more homicides than London and exceeded the total homicides of England and Wales. by 56. In 1918 New York again had six times more homicides than London, and exceeded the total homicides of England and Wales by 67. This contrast cannot be attributed to the peculiar conditions in London induced by the war."

There is much more to the same effect, showing that these conditions are not peculiar to two or three cities, but are characteristic of American cities, and that the showing for theft is at least as bad as that for murder. The figures for robbery are startling. In 1915 New York City reported 838 robberies and assaults with intent to rob where London had 20, in 1916 New York had 886 and London 19, in 1917 New York had 864 and London 38, and in 1918 New York had 849 and London 63.

Do these facts indicate an enforcement of the laws against murder and theft? If not, why is it that we see no organized movement to repeal the whole basic criminal law of the country?

The simple fact is that we do not expect the ordinary laws, the laws of long standing, to be enforced. Some laws are better enforced than those against murder and theft, such as the traffic regulations of our great cities, or the compulsory education laws. Others are presumably less well enforced, as perhaps, the speed laws governing travel on the open highways or the laws against personal smuggling of goods. But no law is perfectly, and very few laws any where near perfectly, enforced. The steady stream of convicts passing in and out of our jails and penitentiaries, the long succession of those found guilty who pay their fines are living witness to this truth. And they represent only a fraction of the failures of law enforcement, for a large proportion of those who commit crimes —Garofalo says at least half—are never caught, and a large proportion of those who are caught are never convicted.

It must be recognized that convictions for crimes, even though they reach one hundred per cent, do not represent law enforcement. Law exists for the purpose of coercing persons to perform certain acts and of restraining them from committing other acts. The effectiveness of the enforcement of a given law is to be judged by the extent to which those who are impelled to neglect a required act, or to perform a forbidden act, are constrained to behave contrary to their impulses. The attachment of penalties to laws implies in advance that infractions are expected to take place. The punishment of violators exists for essentially the same purpose as the law itself, that is, for its preventive or deterrent effect, to keep the forbidden act from being performed. There is no social utility in the punishment of wrong-doers merely for the sake of suffering. Unless a law with its penalties reduces in some measure the frequency of the proscribed behavior, even though convictions and punishments reach one hundred per cent, it were better that the law did not exist. If it does reduce proscribed behavior, with or without convictions and punishments, it is to that extent justified, and may be considered to be, to that extent, enforced.

It is clear, then, that the enforcement of a given law is to be measured not by the absolute number of violations or convictions, nor by the relation of convictions to violations, but by the relation between the frequency with which the act would be committed without the law and the frequency with which it is actually committed under the law. Putting it in personal terms, it is a question of how many people who would indulge in certain behavior in the absence of the law are restrained from such behavior (and how often) because of the law.

Judged in this way, it is safe to say—all the safer because there is no possibility of proof one way or the other—that the prohibition statutes are at least as well enforced as the average of our laws, and much better enforced than the basic laws against murder and theft. The ratio between the number of cases in which liquor is now bought and sold, and the number of cases in which it would be bought and sold without the prohibition laws, is much smaller than the ratio between the actual number of murders and thefts, and the number that would be committed if there were no laws covering those acts.

These statements may seem sufficiently startling. Their justification is to be found in some further consideration of the origin, nature, and functions of criminal law.

The chief objective of organized society, the primary reason for its existence, is the control of individual behavior. In a world of struggle the interests of individuals are always running counter to each other. In numberless ways, the pursuit of unchecked, unmodified impulses by one individual inevitably results in injury, pain, or deprivation to one or more other individuals. Unless individuals can be induced to subordinate their conflicting personal interests to the greater common interests of social cooperation, organized society can not function efficiently, can not, in fact, exist.

In the effort to secure voluntary conformity to social norms society marshals all its resources, enlists all its institutions and sanctions. The family, the church, the school, the press, and the state, however much they may differ in other objectives, are all united in the effort to induce people, consciously or unconsciously, deliberately or automatically, to forego or modify the pursuit of immediate personal impulses and desires in the ways, and to the extent, required for the smooth functioning of the social mechanism of whatever community they belong to.

Every native instinct or impulse that can be directed toward the promotion of conformable behavior is utilized. But among them all, one stands out far exceeding all the others in its practical effectiveness. This is the desire for approbation, frequently in sociological parlance, for want of a better term, called "vanity." The desire for approbation is universal among all normal human beings, and manifests itself in two aspects, the desire for self-approbation, and the desire for the approbation of the group. The two are often inextricably intertwined, particularly as the second is usually indispensable to the first. The first requirement for a good opinion of one's self is the conviction that one enjoys the good opinion of others. From the point of view of social control, therefore, it suffices to confine attention to the desire for the approbation of the group. This approbation of the group inheres in what is usually referred to as public opinion and public sentiment.

From the earliest dawn of self-consciousness upward, our conduct is governed, to an extent unbelieveable until one evaluates it searchingly, for the desire of the good opinion of others. This is the force that determines what kind of clothes we shall wear, what games we shall play, how we shall decorate and adorn ourselves, how our meals shall be ordered, what topics we shall discuss and in what language, to say nothing of the more vital matters included in the moral code itself. The range of this force includes everything between the most rationally controlled volition and the primeval "instinct of the herd." The most remarkable thing about it is that for most people, most of the time, it is sufficient. The great majority of social units, the great bulk of the time, are held to the necessary degree of social conformity by the force of vanity alone.

In an ideal state of society, all social units all of the time would be controlled by vanity, supported and augmented by such other forces as produce willing conformity like altruistic love. This is much the most economical form of social control. It is also much the most pleasant, especially because it is so largely unconscious. But unfortunately it is never completely adequate.

In every society there are always some people, a small minority, who can never, even in the most ordinary exigencies of life, be effectively controlled through vanity and its allied forces. And there is a great majority, approximating totality, who in the more or less aggravating crises of life require something more potent than vanity to hold them to strict conformity. Since these are just the persons and the situations from which the most grievous social injuries are likely to arise, it is imperative that society have at its command some other resources to supplement the mild ones just discussed.

Two such residuary resources are conspicuous in society's arsenal—fear and force. These are normally employed, in the order named, when vanity fails. For certain types of persons, and for certain kinds of temptations, when vanity is impotent fear avails. When fear will not deter, society is compelled to fall back upon its last expedient and compel at least a factual acquiescence by a resort to force.

It is for the employment of fear and force primarily that there has been created that organized aspect of the community that we call the state, the expressed will of which is the law. It is the basic function of the state to apply to the more recalcitrant members of society those agencies of control to which alone they will respond. It is to the state alone—with minor exceptions as in the case of parents and teachers—that the right to use force is exclusively reserved. Consequently, the state can make the most effective use of fear, because it can back up its threats. The development in recent years of many distinctly constructive or regulative functions of the state should not be allowed to obscure its basic character.

The law, then, and par excellence the criminal law, is an explicit description of certain prescribed modes of behavior, conformity to which will be secured when necessary by force if that is possible; if it is not possible to secure complete conformity, then violations will be punished by the forcible infliction of pain or deprivation. As already observed, the provision of penalties indicates that it is not expected in the case of any law that full conformity can be secured even by the most rigorous application of fear and force.

We are accustomed to think of the law, therefore, as a great restraining influence, hedging us about on every side with barriers and restrictions. But the extraordinary truth is that for most of us, most of the time, the law is not a restraining agency at all. It simply does not touch us. The great bulk of the things that the criminal law tells us we must not do, most of us would not do if there were no law whatsoever. Of the readers of this page, there are very few who have ever been restrained from committing anything even approaching a basic crime because there was no law against it. Only a small proportion of the members of an ordinary society ever experience an effective impulse to commit murder, robbery, arson, rape, mayhem, assault and battery, forgery. The great majority of those who do have such impulses would be adequately restrained by vanity if there were no law. And the tragic lesson of centuries of penology is that the small remainder, who are not restrained by their own good impulses nor by vanity, are also not restrained by fear or force, so that the enforcement of law, in so far as it is effected at all, takes the form mainly of mere punishment. Punishment, of course, of certain sorts will effectually restrain the individual concerned for the period of its duration.

The meaning of all this is that most of us, while we conform to the law, are not habituated to *obeying* the law, using *"obey"* in the sense of doing for the sake of the law that which we would not do without it. Some of the more recent forms of laws referred to above—game laws, traffic regulations, sanitary ordinances—have fortunately given us a little education along this line. But they do not touch us very deeply, and have not as yet inclined our hearts to do unhesitatingly and cheerfully that which is inconvenient, distasteful, costly, or even painful just because the law requires it.

Perhaps the closest parallel to the prohibition laws that our legal system affords is that furnished by the customs regulations. Here we are dealing with a type of conduct that has no inherent moral implications at all—the bringing home freely of articles legally acquired in foreign countries. On the contrary, this conduct is of a sort that attracts the very "best" elements in society, the wealthy, the cultured, the moral, the intelligent, the self-respecting. Furthermore, it is conduct which, in the opinion of many of the best informed members of the community—including almost all professional economists—is thoroughly in harmony with social utility as well as personal profit. But it happens to be conduct which the majority of the voters has condemned as prejudicial to the best interests of society, and which is accordingly prohibited by law.

Here, then, is an almost ideal test case. Here is a law that seriously and irritatingly infringes upon personal liberty with reference to conduct that is intrinsically quite blameless. It requires tens of thousands of eminently respectable persons to refrain from doing something, which they are strongly impelled to do, for no other reason on earth than that there is a law against it. What happens? We all know what happens. They do it anyway. That is to say, a very high percentage do it to just the degree that they think they can do it and get away with it. A customs broker of long experience in New York once remarked that there was not a woman living who would not beat the customs if she could. This was doubtless an exaggeration. But who can doubt that the customs laws are so extensively and consistently evaded that if non-enforcement were a valid ground for repeal they ought all be stricken from the books forthwith? If there is any set of laws so badly enforced as to "create disrespect for law" it is these.

The very day after the foregoing words were written, the newspapers announced the existence of a ring of gem smugglers who, according to the estimates, run in diamonds from Antwerp alone to the value of $45,000,-000 annually. At about the same time another newspaper paragraph proclaimed that the smuggling of aliens into this country now exceeds in magnitude the illegal production of liquor—though the item fails to specify on just what basis immigrants and alcohol are compared. But the point is, obviously, if the prohibition statutes must be repealed upon the ground of non-enforcement, why not also the whole immigration law?

It is significant that prohibition is now seldom debated on its merits, that is upon the social desirability of preventing people from drinking intoxicating liquors. Some of the standard lines of attack are summarized below, and their fallacy indicated, in order to throw into high relief the real nature of the predominant objections to the prohibition law.

1. "You can't make people good by law." Of course you can't make people good by law. The purpose of the law is not to make people good, but to make them orderly and harmless. No moral objective should ever be associated with any law. Ordinarily, for the reasons explained, the law runs parallel to the moral code. But the aim of law is not goodness but safety and efficiency. On the whole, laws probably add to the total volume of badness rather than of goodness. For persons who are restrained merely by fear have certainly not acquired any virtue thereby, and those who are not restrained add to the guilt of the act itself the extra guilt of law-breaking.

2. The prohibition laws interfere with personal liberty. Certainly they do. That is the nature of all law. If personal liberty were not inimical to social progress there would be no need of law. The only question is whether, in each particular case, the loss of liberty involved in a given law is more than offset by the gain in social stability, efficiency, order, and security. This must be worked out in each case on its own merits; it cannot be settled by a general dictum. If the gain more than offsets the loss, the law is justified. If it does not, the law should not be passed.

3. The innocent are made to suffer with the guilty;

that is, those whose conduct would be socially innocuous without the law are compelled to go to unnecessary extremes. This, too, is inherent in many forms of law. In the case of game laws, speed regulations, "pistol-toting" laws, etc., it is precisely those conscientious persons who could be trusted to do no harm without the law who will be put to the most inconvenience by their efforts to obey the law, while those who most need the law will continue to do as they please. Here again it is a question of whether the net gain is worth the price.

4. Wholesale violations destroy respect for law. What do you mean by respect for law? It can mean only one of two things. It may mean a willingness to do something that you do not want to do just because the law requires it. According to that definition, violations are an evidence, not a cause, of disrespect for law. Or it may mean a naive faith that the law can be used to make other people do something that they do not want to do. If that is the definition, the sooner we find out what the real potency and limitations of the law are the better. The present situation is undoubtedly helping to reveal the true nature of law. Whether we respect it or not depends upon what we discover it to be.

The real truth, of course, is that every such situation does not *create* disrespect for law, it *reveals* disrespect for law. It shows the law up for what it is, and does the same for a vast number of those who plume themselves on being law-abiding citizens. It shows how lamentably small is the proportion of citizens who will refrain from an act which they regard as both pleasurable and innocent just because it is illegal. They are ready to support enthusiastically those laws that aim to prevent "real criminals" from doing injurious things that they themselves have no effective impulse to do. But the laws that touch them in a tender spot are "unwarranted infringements on personal liberty."

Arguments of this sort are for the most part pure camouflage, or at best what the psychologists nowadays call "rationalizations." Clearing them away lays bare the real ground for most of the clamor for repeal, which is simply this, that millions of perfectly respectable and self-respecting, conscientious, orderly people want to do what the law forbids, and see no earthly harm in doing it. They are habituated to obeying the law for its own sake, and suddenly to do so with respect to a matter of as great interest as the use of alcoholic drinks would require a revolution in their social motivation which they are not prepared to undergo. Consequently they have no intention of obeying the law, yet they dislike thinking of themselves as law-breakers. They are ill at ease in the face of wholesale violations of the law by themselves and others like them. It is not so difficult to put up with a farcical enforcement of the laws against murder, burglary, and arson because the people who break those laws are "bad" people anyway, and not much worse for having broken a law. Furthermore, in so far as any of them are caught and punished that is so much pure gain. But to have a law broken by innumerable "good" people, who thereby incur a certain imputation of badness, is intolerable.

Consequently, the only recourse appears to be to repeal the law. There is doubtless a further incentive in the inconvenience caused to them in their law-breaking by the degree of enforcement that is actually achieved.

The true significance, therefore, of the present Prohibition situation is found in the light that it sheds on the whole position of law in a modern democratic state. There are two main points at issue. The first is the entire question of majority rule. To be sure we often hear it asserted, as another of the stock arguments of the opposition, that the prohibition laws were not passed by a majority but "put across by an organized minority." The answer to this is that all laws, as far as those actively responsible for them are concerned, are passed by minorities. The bulk of the people is never vigorously and positively behind any measure. There can be no doubt that the Prohibition Amendment and the Volstead Act were passed in full accord with our established machinery of legislation, expressly designed to register the will of the majority. We are flatly confronted by the questions, what kind of a government we have, what kind we think we have, and what kind we want to have.

It is too obvious for comment that the smaller the number of people whose impulses are crossed by a given law the less disturbance will the law make, and the better will its enforcement appear to be. But by the same token, the less necessary will such a law be. Granting that the law is justified—that is, that the safety and order secured will more than offset the loss of individual liberty—the more people there are who desire to break it the more necessary it is. The maximum justification for a law would exist if fifty-one per cent of the population perceived rightly that a certain type of behavior was socially beneficial, and forty-nine per cent were unwilling to adopt that line of behavior. But such a law would also involve a maximum difficulty of enforcement. There is no escape from frankly facing the question whether in matters that deeply touch us all we believe in majority rule or not. Are we ready to concede that in certain types of legislation not a simple majority, but a two-thirds, or a three-fourths, or a four-fifths majority shall be required? If so, how shall these types of legislation be determined, and how shall the variable majorities be assigned? Ought the enactment of any new coercive law to be delayed until public opinion and sentiment have developed so far that the law will actually restrain only a small fraction of the population? If so, how small? Are frequent violations of a law legitimate grounds for repealing the law? If so, what is the correct ratio?

Or do we really believe that a majority, even a small majority, has a right to pass a law binding upon the entire group, putting the minority under obligation to obey the law conscientiously, even while working perhaps for its legitimate repeal on reasonable grounds? If so, we can hardly justify the minority in violating the law at will and then using the violations as an argument for repeal. These are questions worthy of the most serious consideration. They lie at the very foundation of our theory of democratic government. The arguments are by no means all on one side. But the answer is vital, for when theory and practice clash, one or the other must be revised or disaster will follow.

The second point illuminated by the present Prohibition situation, closely allied indeed to the one just discussed, is the possibility of developing the directive, regulative, constructive (as contrasted with the repressive and coercive) aspects of the law which, as has been observed, are so characteristic of the modern state and so necessary for the efficient functioning of the modern community. No sociological law is better sustained than the one which declares that *increasing social complexity necessitates increasing social constraint.* There is no doubt that increasing complexity is distinctly characteristic of present social evolution. But there is grave doubt as to whether society will be able to impose the degree and variety of social constraint that are required to keep its own towering edifice from toppling. This constraint will have to do more and more with types of conduct which are intrinsically innocent and devoid of moral implication, but which impede the smooth and orderly functioning of a complicated society, or which threaten the legitimate interests of the various members of such a society. Conformity to this type of constraint will not be supported by any moral scruples nor by any of the ordinary sanctions of "right" behavior. If conceded at all, it must rest either upon a personal appreciation of the social utility of the measure in question—which will probably continue to be deficient among the great mass of the people for a long time to come—or else upon genuine respect for law as law, which means a willingness to obey even though one either does not understand or does not agree.

The prohibition law, rightly interpreted, is exactly a measure of this kind. Its supporters have made a grievous mistake in defending it on moral grounds. As a moral measure Prohibition, just like every other moral legal measure, is indefensible. Its justification, if any, rests upon its necessity as a measure of order, security, efficiency, and the safeguarding of interests. It is not a question whether I consider my neighbor a bad man because he drinks a glass of beer, but whether I have a right to be protected against having a drunken automobile driver run over my child at a street crossing. Individual conduct becomes daily more significant to the welfare of the rest of humanity. In the interests of humanity, therefore, it must be increasingly controlled. The Prohibition law is an exceptionally conspicuous example of this kind of constraint. The true test of its defensibility has already been indicated—if the gain in social security more than offsets the loss in individual liberty then it is a good law, and should be retained. To concede that it must be repealed, *merely because* it can not be enforced is to confess our society bankrupt of the resources indispensable for its own future protection and maintenance.

In the last analysis, however, it must not be forgotten that control by law is the most expensive, painful, and generally unsatisfactory form of control that society exercises. The goal of intelligent social engineering should be to reduce it to a minimum, supplanting it by control through vanity, love in its various forms, and any other appeal that will produce voluntary conformity. As a part of this program, sanctions must be built up in favor of law-abidingness itself. In some way or other conscientious people must be made to feel the same social condemnation for the violation of a law that they now do for a breach of the moral code. Only in this way will the society of the future be able to maintain the operation of the increasing system of regulative laws which will be necessary for its existence, and at the same time avoid the harsh, irritating, and socially disruptive measures which accompany the enforcement of law by resort to fear and force. To defend the repeal of any regulative law on the ground that it does not express the moral conviction of a great proportion, even a majority of people, or that it interferes with the enjoyment of personal liberty, or that it is not perfectly enforced, is to pave the way for a more disastrous social chaos than is likely to result from the wildest lucubrations of the reddest radical who was ever deported to Russia.

5

POPULARITY V. PEDAGOGY

Written in 1919

To a friend of mine who had just achieved his Ph. D. and was about to enter upon his career as a teacher, the mother-in-law of a very eminent college professor remarked, "Of course, the best young men do not go into the teaching profession nowadays." However much he might question her tact, my friend did not feel that he could gainsay the truth of her statement.

For some years past, and now particularly since the war has focussed criticism on all social institutions, there has been a large amount of pondering and discussion as to what is the matter with the teaching profession. Whether or not it be true that none of the very best young men are still entering it, there is not the least doubt that for some time it has been attracting a startlingly small proportion of the ablest, most ambitious, and most promising graduates of our schools of higher learning. Those who believe that education is an essential of a progressive civilization and a sound democracy are justifiably alarmed at the vision of the type of men and women into whose hands this responsibility is falling.

Assuming the gravity of the situation, the first step toward a solution is a careful investigation into the causes. It would be idle to seek to find a single cause which would furnish a comprehensive explanation. Social facts of the magnitude and complexity of this never have a single cause. There is doubtless an element of truth in each of the various factors which are customarily cited, particularly the low range of salaries which prevails in the profession. Too much weight can not, however, be given to the matter of salaries, for two reasons. In the first place, there is no reason to believe that the fund of idealism and self-sacrifice has run so low among the young people of today as to prevent an adequate number from taking up teaching if the profession offered the other rewards of honor, dignity, and service which would compensate for the small pecuniary return. In the second place, low salaries are themselves a secondary cause, and it remains to be explained why education has fallen so low in value as to command such a meagre remuneration for its purveyors.

Out of many possible partial causes I wish to select for emphasis one which is unquestionably fundamental. The matter with teaching is that there are no concrete and tangible criteria of its success. In the long run, ambitious and capable young people will avoid an occupation if there is grave doubt that ability, faithfulness and achievement will fail to receive recognition and some form of appropriate reward. In almost every occupation there are positive and easily applied tests of success, upon the result of which rewards will be, or at least can be, based. This is, of course, particularly true of those occupations which we group under the head of "business." The purpose of business, in itself, is to make money, and the successful business man is the one who makes money. The degree of his success is almost mathematically proportioned to the amount of money he makes.

When we turn to other lines of work such as the professions, particularly where the element of altruism or public service enters in, the standards of success become somewhat less definite. But even in the professions there is usually something positive to go by. The teaching profession stands almost alone, with the exception of the ministry—a companionship which lends weight to the argument. The function of a civil engineer is to build railways and bridges, and if he builds good railways and bridges he is a good engineer. A lawyer's business is to win cases, and a positive decision is passed upon each of his efforts. A doctor's mission is to maintain health, cure disease, and prevent death, and we know whether or not he does so in a fair proportion of his cases.

The business of the teacher can be described only as teaching—or as education, which is equally vague. Who knows, or how can we tell, whether a given teacher is doing his job well or not? There are two chief reasons why it is impossible to judge with certainty whether or not a given individual is doing good teaching. The first is that there is no general agreement as to what the real purpose of education is. The current literature is full of heated and learned discussions of the subject, but the matter remains unsettled. We do not know whether the purpose of education is to train people to think, or to fit them for a definite life-work, or to supply them with an amount of knowledge, or to give them "culture." This obviously applies with greatest force to what may be called "general" education—the brand of education supplied by the ordinary academic college course. In this respect the teacher in a technical school has a decided advantage over the college instructor, for the former may eventually be judged by the performance of his pupils. I do not propose to enter into this phase of the subject further than to emphasize the fact that until we can answer the question, "Why is a teacher?" we are quite unprepared to approach the problem, "What is a good teacher?"

The second difficulty in appraising the work of a teacher is that, even supposing we know what we want from him, we have no way of telling whether he is delivering the goods. I shall develop this point particularly with reference to the college teacher. There are two conceivable criteria of the success of the teacher—product and performance. If either of these furnished a tangible and reliable basis of judgment, it would be possible to measure the ability or success of the teacher. But neither of them does. The major difficulty in passing upon the product of a teacher is that just mentioned—we do not know what we expect of him. His product is, or should be, educated young men and women. But we are incapable of measuring or grading the education possessed by any group of graduates. The second difficulty is that even assuming that the product can be appraised after a fashion it is almost impossible under modern conditions to tell to what extent, or in what degree, that product may be credited to the efforts of any given teacher.

The raw material upon which the teacher works is composed of young men and women. They come within his sphere of influence as freshmen and leave it as graduates. In the larger institutions an individual teacher touches only a fraction of the student body, and those only in one or two of the college years, and in a single subject. There is no conceivable set of tests whereby power of thought, culture, or general education in the graduate may be traced back to its original source in the individual teacher. The product of an educational institution is the composite of the efforts of all the members of the faculty and all those varied and immaterial influences which go to make up the atmosphere and power of the institution.

The one form, or aspect, of education wherein it might theoretically be possible to measure the success of the teacher is the accumulation of facts. It is conceivable that those whose business it is to pass upon the success of the teacher might themselves conduct examinations to determine the degree to which his pupils had mastered the subject. But experience and sound common sense long ago discredited this practice, and the only examinations ordinarily given are those set and graded by the teacher himself.

The trouble with examinations, as we all know, is that they are almost worse than useless as a test of the success of the teacher—to say nothing of the accomplishment of the pupils. There are plenty of teachers who are experts in fitting candidates to pass examinations, but whose teaching does not last twenty-four hours after the test. I have in mind a teacher, reputed to be most successful, whose students say of him that he gives them explicit and definite facts in a very clear way, and then rigidly requires them to give them back in exactly the same form. But if this were in fact this teacher's sole claim to greatness, how paltry would his achievement be! I am reminded of Dr. Saleeby's vigorous if inelegant indictment of our whole educational system: "A simple analogy will show the disastrous character of the present process, which may be briefly described as 'education' by cram and emetic. It is as if you filled a child's stomach to repletion with marbles, pieces of coal and similar material incapable of digestion—the more worthless the material the more accurate the analogy: then applied an emetic and estimated your success by the completeness with which everything was returned, more especially if it was returned 'unchanged,' as the doctors say. Just so do we cram the child's mental stomach, its memory, with a selection of dead facts of history and the like (at least when they are not fictions) and then apply a violent emetic called an examination (which like most emetics causes much depression) and estimate our success by the number of statements which the child vomits on the examination paper—if the reader will excuse me. Further if we are what we usually are, we prefer that the statements shall come back 'unchanged'—showing no signs of mental digestion. We call this 'training the memory.'" [1]

If the success of teaching lay in packing the mind with facts, what a pathetic failure the whole business would be, anyway! How many of the facts, how much of the knowledge, acquired through a college course remain to the day of graduation, to say nothing of five years later? (If you have any doubts on the subject, gentle and educated reader, get a copy of the entrance examinations of one of our universities or of the College Entrance Board, and try to figure out what would be your chance of passing it.)

Perhaps the nearest approach to a real measure of this

1. Parenthood and Race Culture, p. 121.

conception of teaching is found when one course follows another, so that the pupils come well or ill prepared—prepared for the same sort of thing.

The effort to evaluate the success of the teacher on the basis of his performance under prevailing conditions is even more hopeless. The underlying fact is that no one knows anything at first hand about a teacher's teaching except his pupils themselves. As one of my friends puts it, the teacher alone of all professional men has no opportunity to perform before his peers. It is universally conceded that official visits to the classroom by superior college officers introduce such an artificial and unnatural atmosphere as to be almost worse than useless. The teacher works normally only in the presence of his raw material. This being the case, it comes about that all contemporary judgment of an individual's teaching traces back ultimately to the undergraduates. Extreme as it may seem, this statement will bear examination. Opinions otherwise formed will be found, upon analysis, to rest upon his writings or other work, his participation in various college activities, or, most frequently of all, his general personality. These, of course, are no judgments of teaching whatever, though perhaps, pragmatically, they are as safe a guide to the ability of a teacher as any now available.

If the undergraduates were sound judges of what constitutes good teaching, satisfactory procedure might be based upon their opinion. Unfortunately, they are not, and it is unfair to expect them to be. If the philosophers, the pedagogists, and the college presidents can not decide as to the purpose of education, we ought not to look for final judgment to the undergraduates. The average college student knows whether or not he likes a given teacher and that is about as far as he goes. He does not attempt to analyze the grounds upon which his like or dislike is based.

I well remember reading in the Atlantic Monthly, some years ago, a plaintive lamentation from Mr. Crothers that in his boyhood days he used to lie awake nights fearing that he wouldn't have his lessons to suit his teacher, while now the teacher lies awake fearing that he (I believe Mr. Crothers said "she") may not make the lesson interesting to the pupils. In the years that have intervened the matter has progressed to the point where it is not enough that the teacher be interesting—he must also be amusing. There are many ways known to the experienced teacher of winning popularity among the students which have no connection with good teaching. To cite a single instance, I recall the case of a new teacher in one of our most honored institutions who was soberly advised by one of the older members of the faculty that if he wished to be popular he must plan to give cuts every so often.

Take them by and large, undergraduates will account a teacher good if they enjoy his courses, if they look forward to the hour in his classroom with pleasure, and advise their sub-class friends to take his subjects. They do not stop nicely to discriminate as to whether their pleasure in the course is due to the ability of the teacher to make them think, to arouse interest in his subject, to train their minds, or to divert and entertain them for fifty minutes. The rare individual who is happily gifted with all of these qualities is almost certain to be popular, and in his case student opinion is probably sound. But as between the man who can really inspire, stimulate, and instruct, and the one who is facile in entertainment, the students as a whole are unsafe judges. Student opinion, moreover, is tremendously subject to fads and fancies, oftentimes of a very whimsical and irrational character. Almost inconceivably trivial factors enter into the students' appraisal of a course. It is a positive fact that the success or failure of a course may depend upon whether it is held on the first or third floor, or whether it comes at 9:30 A. M. or 3:00 P.M. Many other fortuitous elements may enter in, such as conflict with other courses, grouping of courses in majors and minors, and the like.

The upshot of the matter is that the faculty is subject to the undergraduates, and the students really choose the teachers. The college officer or officers whose duty it is to recommend teachers for reappointment or promotion must pass judgment upon the success of the individual's teaching. How shall they proceed? Assuming that the recommendation must be made by a committee and that this committee has given careful consideration as to what constitutes good teaching—for example, whether it consists in keeping above the margin of positive failure the stupid and slow individuals, or interesting and holding the great mass of average men, or developing and inspiring the rare and gifted spirits—still in the end the committee is dependent for its evidence upon the judgments of the undergraduates.

Now, bad as the case is, it would not be so utterly hopeless if the committee would recognize the situation frankly, take the bull by the horns, and set out deliberately to secure a balanced, sound, and fair student opinion of the man. If a sufficient number of representative students were frankly asked to state their opinions, being fully impressed with the seriousness of the occasion, the resulting judgment might not be so far astray. Naturally, this method is not adopted. Instead of it the committee begins by recalling all that they have heard about the man's teaching. Then other members of the faculty and college authorities are consulted. The reports of these individuals are treated as their own opinions. But they are not. Like the opinions of the committee itself, they are the reflected judgments of the undergraduates, only passed through one more stage. A sentiment which originates from an unsound source does not gain in reliability by remoteness from that source. As far as the teacher's performance is concerned, therefore, the investigation of the committee can be practically nothing more than the collection of evidences of student opinion transmuted into different forms. In the matter of the success of a teacher, scientific men will accept a decision reached by methods of investigation which they would not tolerate for a moment in their laboratories. Any independent estimates of the teacher, as I have suggested, are not based upon his teaching but upon his general personality, the figures showing the size and growth of his classes—the one universal criterion, especially under the elective system—the percentage of failures, or the average of grades.

The young teacher is, therefore, subjected to a system (or lack of it) which can only be described as government by gossip. His reputation—as far as teaching goes—is only the reflection of campus rumors. And of all gossip, possibly campus gossip is the least reliable. Like all gossip, it is not always false. Many a teacher adjudged successful by prevailing methods would be found so by the application of the most scientific tests. But campus gossip is assuredly a feeble reed to lean upon as the chief support for administrative action. Criticism is dear to human nature. Half a dozen students who are displeased with a teacher's manners or methods will create more of an impression than a couple of hundred who are satisfied and, therefore, not moved to speak. A teacher with a positive personality who antagonizes a few while pleasing many may suffer in reputation compared with a drab individual who does not arouse any definite reaction in his pupils. In the student's mind, disagreement with a teacher is prone to be confused with a low estimate of his ability. This is particularly true when the subject taught is one which leaves room for legitimate differences of opinion. "I don't agree with Professor Brown" easily becomes transmuted into "I don't like Professor Brown" or "Brown's course is no good." The teacher, therefore, who arouses the most positive reactions in his pupils, who makes it a point to prick them into independent thought, is the very one most likely to arouse unfavorable comment. I have in mind the case of a teacher who was forced out of a college by the hostile and contemptuous attitude of his students. Yet when it was known that he was going, many a student was heard to remark that he was the most brilliant, inspiring, or suggestive man he had ever studied under. Arguments of this kind are frequently met with the reply that while all this is true of undergraduate opinion, yet time brings wiser counsel, and the judgment of the alumni is on the whole sound and accurate. True enough. That is why I said contemporary judgment in an earlier paragraph. But the opinion of the alumni has but little weight in practical decisions about faculty promotions compared with that of the student body. It is diffused and inchoate. It makes but a faint impact on the ear of faculty or administration compared to campus gossip. Worst of all, it comes too late. Ten years is certainly not too much to allow for the graduate to attain the necessary perspective and begin to evaluate accurately the contribution to his development made by his various college teachers. But the first ten years of a teacher's career are the critical and determinative ones as far as his advancement and recognition are concerned. Long before the students, whom he perhaps met as freshmen or sophomores, have had time to form ripe judgments of his influence upon their lives and characters, he has met the successive crises of his career, and if he be not fortunate enough to have enjoyed a favorable contemporary reputation, has either passed on to some other institution, or been relegated to one of the inferior academic categories out of which it is most difficult to emerge. In these facts we find one justification—almost the only one—for the large importance customarily given to research or publication in determining the claims of a teacher to promotion. It is a tacit admission of the impotence of college authorities to correctly appraise true teaching ability. In his publications a man may be judged by his peers. Here is tangible evidence of his mental ability, his powers of analysis and expression, his attitude toward his subject—in brief, his whole intellectual equipment. We can at least tell whether the man has brains. Unfortunately for the interests of education, achievements in research and success in teaching are not only not parallel or complementary, they are often antagonistic. The recent vigorous revulsion against research as a basis for academic recognition is well founded. What the buyers of education want is teaching, not publication.

The inadequacy of existing methods to determine true teaching ability is strikingly portrayed in the report of a committee, of which President James, of the University of Illinois, was the chairman, entitled Methods of Discovering the Exceptional Teacher. This report, which deserves wider acquaintance than it has received, is based upon the answers to a questionnaire sent out to a number of college administrators, asking them to describe the methods by which they judged the ability of the members of their teaching staff. The general conclusion was a frank confession that no reliable and workable system of tests exists or is in operation at the present time.

I remarked above that the low salary scale in the teaching profession is only a secondary explanation of the low quality of teachers. In fact, it is probable that just this impossibility of gauging accurately the success of teachers accounts in large measure for the small financial estimate placed upon their labors. No one cares to pay heavily for something the quality of which is uncertain. Since we can not tell who the good teachers are, and suspect that a very considerable proportion of the lot are poor teachers, we do not care to pass out liberal compensations to the profession as a whole. I strongly suspect that if the purchasing public could know for certain when it was getting the genuine article in education it would be willing to pay for it handsomely. In this connection, contrast the pay of college professors with the remuneration of teachers in preparatory and tutoring schools, or the earnings of private tutors. These men have a definite object to accomplish—to get the boy into college, or through the examination. Their activities may or may not come under the head of education, but they are directed toward a definite end, which is desired and can be recognized by the parents. The teacher who can accomplish this end with a uniform degree of success can almost name his own salary.

One more point. The life of a teacher is a pleasant one, and may be a very easy one. It has many compensations apart from its monetary returns. Consequently, it attracts many young men and women who are not dependent upon their earnings for material comforts, and are glad to accept teaching positions at nominal salaries. To hold good positions they must, of course, have some degree of mental ability. But it is not at all necessary that they be really able teachers. Because of the impossibility of properly differentiating between different grades of teaching ability the large numbers of teachers of this class offer a discouraging and deadening competition to young people who are dependent upon their earnings. Their teaching is good enough according to prevailing tests, they lend an air of grace and well-being to the college atmosphere, they are able to participate in activities of many sorts which cost money and which add to their standing in the community, they are able to carry out lines of research closed to the impecunious teacher, and they can afford to wait for promotions even though they be long in coming. It needs no demonstration to show how the presence of this class of teachers, interfering with the normal play of supply and demand, makes it unnecessary for the public to pay as highly for education even as it would be willing to.

To the college graduate, looking over the field of possible occupations before making his choice, the teaching profession presents many attractions. It is stimulating, interesting, honorable, and broadening, at its best. But more or less intuitively or subconsciously, without analysis, he realizes that in the teaching profession there is no certainty that true merit and ability will receive its due reward either in money or other emoluments, while there is absolute certainty that even marked and recognized ability will never receive more than a beggarly financial compensation. He senses the rather commiserating, patronizing attitude of the general public toward the teaching profession as a whole, and he turns to some occupation where the rewards of talent, industry, and achievement are not only larger, but more sure.

It is not my purpose to seek to suggest a remedy for this deplorable situation. In truth the outlook seems decidedly dark. A reduction of the elective system might accomplish something, particularly by lessening the importance of numbers of students or size of classes in judging the success of a teacher. The free elective system undoubtedly tends to throw the determination of the curriculum into the hands of the students. It also aggravates the tendency to commit the choice of the faculty to the same arbiters. But prescribed courses alone will not solve the problem of grading teachers. In fact, in some respects the situation might be even worse. For pupils forced to take subjects that they did not want would be prone to vent their feelings in criticisms of the teacher.

Possibly some alleviation might be found in taking a leaf from the book of industrial concerns and introducing a personnel department into our universities. This department would be composed of persons qualified by nature and training to judge human nature, and to devise and apply methods of judging teaching ability. They would be experts in educational appraisement. It is one of the curious traditions of the educational world that a teacher of a given subject can properly be judged only by other teachers in the same subject. It is true that a man's reputation as a scholar or research man will be most familiar to teachers in the corresponding department, but the same does not follow of his teaching ability. There is no reason why a teacher of Greek can not be as accurately judged, as far as his teaching ability goes, by a teacher of mathematics or any other subject as by another teacher of Greek. The best judge of all may very likely be some one who has never taught a day in his life. This is the principle back of all the modern employment systems of industrial and commercial concerns. The appraisement of vocational aptitudes is an art, or a science, by itself. In a university, such a personnel board would naturally turn to the faculties of the various departments for such information. But that would be only a portion of the criteria upon which the final solution was based.

But whatever the solution, some solution there must be before there can be an approach to the establishment of better educational conditions. There is almost universal agreement that the keystone, the core, the heart of all education is the teacher. Before we can have good education we must be able to recognize, select, and reward good teachers.

6

BUSINESS AS AN INSTITUTION

Written in 1937

WHEN FRANKLIN D. ROOSEVELT assumed the chair of office in 1933 he proceeded to set up what was probably the most academic and literate administration in the history of the nation. As we are all aware, this came to be known as the "Brain Trust." It was notable for many things, among them the unquestioned ability and high spirit of industry and devotion manifested by the group as a whole. But one feature, which is of especial interest to the group gathered here this evening, was the surprisingly small number of professional sociologists included in the official family. There were a few notable exceptions, some of whom, as we know, found the atmosphere not entirely congenial and voluntarily withdrew. But viewing the situation as a whole it is a striking fact that in a vast enterprise, which was essentially sociological in its nature, an almost negligible part of the responsibility was entrusted to those who had made sociology their life study and work.

What reasons can we discern for this situation?

To begin with, I presume that very few professional

sociologists, particularly in the presence of such an eminent gathering of their colleagues from the allied social sciences, would admit that the determinative factor was an inferior level of ability or scientific attainment on the part of sociologists as compared with economists, political scientists, and financiers. There may have been some influence of the President's individual background and personal acquaintanceships. But it seems quite clear to me that the outstanding explanation is to be found in the fact that the emergency which confronted President Roosevelt was commonly regarded by the public, and doubtless by the President himself, as an "economic" situation, and of course economic matters should be dealt with by economists first of all. In other words, the President's conduct is simply an unusually conspicuous example of the familiar line of distinction drawn between economics and sociology. Tonight I should like to raise certain questions in this connection. Is this line of demarcation valid? Are economics and sociology two distinct sciences (or, perhaps, is one a science and the other some other kind of discipline) like two neighbors who have a polite bowing acquaintance and pass the time of day over a sturdy boundary fence, but each of whom would vigorously resent any trespass of the other upon his territory? Or do they possibly represent two different approaches to the same great body of social fact? Or, finally, is it the function of sociology to deal specifically with certain aspects of this body of social fact, while economics confines itself to other aspects?

I have no expectation or ambition to answer these questions categorically in the next few minutes. All I wish to do is to suggest certain considerations which may throw some light upon the problem, and may not only clarify our thinking on the subject, but may also possibly make some slight contribution to a more constructive and comprehensive application of sociological theory to some of the emergent problems of contemporary life.

First of all, we may take it as a matter of course that economics deals with the particular departments of the social organization which are concerned with the production, distribution, and exchange of wealth, and of useful services. Fundamentally, as the conventional definitions of "wealth" indicate, economics concentrates upon the provision of those material supplies upon which human life and happiness depend. Such attention as it devotes to personal services is largely conditioned by the principles which it has derived from the study of the material aspects of civilization. The first question that arises, therefore, is whether the administration of material interests has about it some peculiar quality that puts it in a different category from the administration of educational, recreational or reproductional interests, causing the latter group to be fit subject for sociological consideration and interpretation, but barring the first. It would be difficult, indeed, to find any logical justification for such a conclusion. The material interests of life are at least as basic as the procreational and recreational. They involve at least as much social integration and social control. They have at least as many distinct processes. They are at least as closely tied up with social change, and they just as frequently manifest social lag. Why, then, has sociology been so modest and timid about including them in the full scope of its theoretical inquiry?

One reason seems to stand out conspicuously and obviously. This is, simply, that economics got on to the ground first, staked out a claim, and put up unmistakable trespass signs on all sides. This, again, was a perfectly natural and comprehensible development. The material interests of life are not only basic; they are objective, tangible, and observable. Adam Smith's famous story of the pins is something that everybody can understand. Moreover, many of the materials with which economics deals are measurable by everyday quantitative instruments. They can be counted, weighed, and handled accurately by mathematical and statistical processes. They lend themselves to the construction of a science which, in its primary aspects, has every appearance of precision, accuracy and uniformity. To the extent that economics confines itself to these phases of its field it can be both convincing and sound. It is only when it follows its own analyses into the profounder realms of human relationships, and the factors of individual interests and behavior that lie back of them, that it becomes vague and equivocal, not to say unrealistic. The more penetrating and analytical economists have always discovered that sooner or later their search for relationships led them to the behavior of the individual man. They could not adequately interpret the group phenomena which concerned them unless they knew something about the character and motivation of personal conduct. Unfortunately, at the time when the ground work of economic theory was being laid, there was no competent psychology to answer the questions that scholarly economists were asking. There was no developed science to tell them what the social unit is really like in his dynamic characteristics, or why he acts as he does. Consequently, for the rounding out of their theory, they had to postulate a social unit, which has come to be familiarly known as the "economic man," and who has played his central role in economic theory from that time down to very recent years, and still holds an important place. By the time sociology began tardily to mature itself into a self-respecting scientific discipline the structure of economics had become so well integrated, and had achieved for itself such a large and well merited measure of social recognition and esteem, that the new science naturally felt reluctant to invade the field. It was not sure of its own ground, it could offer no well authenticated laws to supplant or qualify those of economics, and it was justifiably reluctant about seeming to rush in where scholarly angels had trod for so long. By a certain sort of unwritten Gentlemen's Agreement it confined itself to elaborate and comprehensive inquiries into, and interpretations of, those human relationships that had to do with sex, the family, recreation, the political organization, education, and innumerable minor interests, but left the great field of the provision of material needs pretty severely alone.

Natural though this development has been, it seems to me that its consequences have been unfortunate for both economics and sociology. Economics has missed the humanizing influence and the sense of realism that could be derived only from the truly sociological handling of its materials, while sociology has not only suffered a mutilation through the loss of an essential member, but even within the fields which it has developed has missed the enrichment and completeness of its own theory which could have been derived from a thorough study of economic relationships.

It seems to me that the time is now ripe to correct this lesion, and to bring about such a rapprochement of the two sciences as shall serve to round out and solidify them both. It seems to me that the key to this rapprochement is to be found in the concept of business, and it is to that concept that I invite your attention for the next few minutes. Business is one of those common words which are used in everyday conversation, but which are also indispensable for the analysis of social science, unless some artificial word is arbitrarily put in their place. Everybody talks about business, and a great many people engage in what they believe to be business, and yet very few people could tell precisely what they mean by business. This lack is directly traceable to sociology, for business, as I am thinking of it, is essentially a sociological reality, and should be clarified by sociological methodology. Yet most sociological writers seem to have caught almost no glimpse of its real meaning, and to ignore it almost completely. In preparation for this talk I looked over a number of the leading textbooks in sociology—those which happened to be on my own shelves—to see to what extent they gave recognition to business as a sociological concept. I was interested to discover that out of twenty-one books examined, eleven did not include business in their indexes, seven listed the word, and three made a qualified mention, such as "business ethics," or something of the sort. There was not one that gave more than a passing discussion of business, and none that seemed to recognize business in the way which I believe to be sound and essential. This is as an institution. (Incidentally, there are a number of these texts that do not list "institution" in their indexes.) Many of these books deal with the Industrial Revolution and its consequences, and to some extent with labor, wages, and the employer-employee relationship. But the treatment is invariably scanty and almost casual.

There is, of course, a great deal of difference of

opinion among sociologists as to the definition and meaning of institution. It would be futile for me to attempt to consolidate that concept as a preliminary to a discussion of business. But I think you will understand what I have in mind when I say that by an institution I understand such social constructs as the state, the church, the family, the school, the press, the law—a kind of grouping that will be perfectly familiar to you all. The point that I wish to make is that business has a logical place in any such category, and should stand on a par with the most important items such as the family and the state. I must confess that I was considerably surprised when I discovered that the voluminous Sumner-Keller "Science of Society" is among those works that does not include business in its index. Knowing the large place that Sumner gave to the "self-maintenance of society" one might expect him to have given exceptional recognition to business, even though his major interest was in the elemental and more primitive aspects of social organization. How completely his treatment ignores modern economic relationships is revealed by the fact that this index lacks not only business, but such related words as "corporation," "bond," "stock," and "profits." Is not a corporation bond just as truly a sociological reality as a kinship bond? Is a certificate of stock any less of a sociological document than a marriage certificate?

What then is business in a sociological sense and what claim has it to be considered as an institution? In spite of the great divergence that I have mentioned, there is a fairly general agreement among sociologists that an institution is an established integration of social elements for the satisfaction of some major interest, including in elements not only certain tangible equipment, but more fundamentally relationships and established modes of social procedure. I repeat that if you will think of the family, the state, and the church, as institutions, you will have a preliminary idea of what I mean by a business. More specifically, by a business I mean the organization of social elements into a unit designed for the production and supplying of material goods and certain types of personal services. Its essential earmark is the integration of two or more social elements. Let me make this clear by starting with a situation with which we are all familiar. We are well aware that we live in what is called a capitalistic system, and that economic goods are produced and distributed according to the characteristics of such a system. We also recognize that the outstanding feature of this system is a group of productive units composed of a group of distinct factors, among which capital tends to be predominant. We are indebted to economic theory for a clear exposition of what these factors are. As we all know in addition to capital these factors are land, labor, and organization or management. A large part of economic theory devotes itself to an exposition of the relationships between these various factors, and the way in which the eventual product is distributed among them. What economics has failed to perceive clearly is that the integration itself is a distinct entity, quite apart from any or all of these factors that compose it. One evidence of this failure is that economics has provided no word to designate any such entity, and we are forced to adopt the word business in lieu of any more precise technical term. The basic reason why economics has failed to clarify this situation is that business, as a distinct integration of a group of factors, is a sociological concept, not an economic one. The thing that is essential is the accepted, established, or socially authorized mode of correlating various social elements into a functioning unit. Only sociology is by its nature competent to investigate or understand this kind of a human nexus.

Let us illustrate this by considering the modern corporation. This product of social evolution is clearly recognized in economics, and some of its aspects are elaborately dealt with. There is a whole library of books on corporation finance, on stocks, bonds, as well as on the relationships between corporations as employers, and laborers, landlords, and customers. But one would search far to find any illuminating discussion of what the corporation itself is as a functioning unit. It is partly for this reason that the economic treatment of profits, elaborate and diversified as it is in the various textbooks, is so inconclusive and vague. The reason for this is that the very essence of a corporation is ownership, and ownership is a sociological concept just as truly as domination, submission, exploitation, or any other item in the long lists with which you are familiar. It is really amazing when one runs through a number of the best economic textbooks, to find how little recognition is given to ownership, and how little space devoted to its interpretation. The explanation, I repeat, is primarily that the nature of ownership is sociological, and that most economists, rightly enough, have not even appreciated the necessity of investigating it.

What is true of the corporation is true of various other types of productive units. Every society has its own characteristic mode of organizing the essential factors of production into functioning units. These typical units not only determine the manner whereby needful goods are supplied to the population, but also give color to the whole social structure. This may seem to be only another way of recognizing that the economic mores are dominant, as Sumner so often pointed out, or of making a bow to economic determinism, This is neither here nor there. The essential point is that in the economic organization of society there are certain features which are so definitely a matter of social relationship, motivation, and process that they can be dealt with adequately only by sociological techniques. In other words, they are to be approached just as any other great institution is approached, and to be incorporated in sociological theory on a par with the family, the state, or the school.

As a single illustration of the confusion and practical futility that result from the failure to recognize business as an institution we may cite the familiar myth of the "efficiency of American business." When business is viewed properly as an institution, that is, as an integrated nexus of social elements designed to serve a human need, we realize that it is not business, but technology, that is efficient. American scientists, engineers, and technologists in general, have developed a truly amazing set of instrumentalities for the production and physical handling of material goods. But the group of social institutions which is supposed to secure the abundance, wide distribution, and satisfying use of these goods—and this is business—must be recognized as a lamentable and tragic failure.

Such a recognition of business as an institution will not in any way infringe upon the vested academic interests of economists, nor detract in the slightest from the majesty and utility of that science. On the contrary, if properly conducted it should simply afford economics the materials for making itself richer, sounder, and more conclusive in many ways. There is a vast special field of economic interpretation into which the sociologist as such has no call to enter. But he has both the right and the obligation to offer certain contributions, just as the great sciences of biology and psychology are under obligation to furnish materials to the sociologist without which his own work must be meager and unsatisfactory.

For the sociologist himself, this recognition of business as an institution, and the adequate exploration of its meaning, will not only complete and stabilize economic theory, but will equip sociology far more adequately to make useful applications of its own theory to the needs of the contemporary world. For it is indubitably evident that a large portion of the anomalies and futilities of the contemporary social structure are essentially economic in their character, and that only as sociological interpretations and techniques are made available can the faults in either structure or function be corrected, and the full values be derived from the existing social equipment and endowment which are the legitimate goals of the applied branches of every science.

7

MACHINES V. MEN

Written in 1931

IN THE early months of 1930 newspapers reports described President Hoover as very much worried over the accumulated wheat surplus, which amounted to about one hundred and fifty million bushels, and was increasing every year. The Department of Agriculture was simultaneously sending out a staff of experts to attempt to persuade the farmers of the Northwest to plant two million acres less of wheat. At the same time, in New York City, thousands of men were gathering daily in bread lines on the Bowery, standing for hours in the cold and rain waiting for a chance to get a ticket which would entitle them to stand in another line for more hours in the hope of receiving eventually a cup of coffee and a few slices of bread and butter.

In the succeeding months the wheat surplus has continued to pile up—two hundred and sixty-five million bushels in August—and the bread lines have grown conspicuously longer and more numerous.

What is true of wheat is true of other agricultural produce, and what is true of agricultural produce is also true of the products of factories, and of machine industry in general. On every hand we hear the cry of "overproduction" and on every street-corner there are men begging for food and shelter. Some agitators call it a "Buyers' Strike" and start "Buy Now" campaigns, and Mr. William Trufant Foster tells us that our troubles would disappear if each of us would spend five dollars a week more for two weeks. On the other hand Mr. J. W. Barton told the bankers recently convening at Cleveland that our standard of living is too high and should be lowered—that is, that we should buy less.

Everybody agrees that the capacity of our productive plant is far in excess of our ability to consume, and nobody denies that millions of men and women and children are hungry, and desolate, and growing desperate.

If we knew of such things only through reading the descriptions of travelers in strange foreign parts, we could scarcely believe them. They are too incredible. Alice in Wonderland, in all her topsy-turvy world, never saw anything so absurd, so contradictory, so illogical, so completely upside down.

At the present moment, the external features of the situation are crystallizing in the phenomenon we call "unemployment." There is a tendency to approach unemployment as a detached matter, and to discuss remedies and preventives in terms of specifics for an isolated disease. In fact, unemployment is only one aspect of a complex, far-reaching social situation, closely related to the financial depression, the agricultural and industrial surplus, the decline of the textile industry in New England, the menace of the next war, and numerous other more or less conspicuous evils.

At the same time, while unemployment is only one

phase of the total situation, it is an important and illuminating phase, and a thorough grasp of the causative factors that lie back of unemployment will conduce to a clearer understanding of all the related ills, and help to point the way to remedies that will really get at the root of the whole chaotic complex. It is the purpose of this paper to set forth some of the chief factors in the unemployment situation, about which there is really nothing mysterious, intricate, or abstruse. On the contrary, the failure to understand unemployment is due largely to the difficulty of perceiving the significance of the familiar and commonplace.

I

First of all, it is necessary to come to a fairly definite understanding as to what is meant by unemployment. Of course, unemployment is being "out of work." But this is not enough. More than half of the population is out of work all the time, and all of the population is out of work more than half of the time. Only certain persons are supposed to work, and these are supposed to work only part of the time. It immediately appears that the meaning of unemployment is conditioned by the particular social structure and conventions of any society. Only those persons can be unemployed who are normally supposed to be at work, and these can be unemployed only during the hours when they are normally supposed to be at work. In such a country as the United States this immediately eliminates all persons under fourteen or sixteen years of age.

But not all of the adult population is supposed to be at work. It is not a part of our social system, in the first place, that married women should work. Many of them have to, but it is tacitly assumed that it is a situation from which they will escape as soon as their husbands' incomes make it possible. We would never think of applying the term unemployed to the wife of a prosperous business man, if she devotes her time to bridge, dancing, and charity—or even if she does not. Nor do we expect all children above fourteen to be at work; in fact, we rather smugly assume that they will not be, and shut our eyes to the vast numbers of them who are.

But still further eliminations must be made. Not all husbands, or heads of families, are necessarily supposed to work. The label of unemployment would be most incongruous if applied to a wealthy man who sees fit to live on his income without doing a stroke of work, nor is it ordinarily applied to the independent business man who closes his shop or shuts down his factory during a period of dull trade. Indeed, the term is not ordinarily used in connection with independent producers of any kind.

Without unduly prolonging this process of elimination, it becomes clear that the term unemployment, in its customary use, applies exclusively to hired workers, wage earners, persons who expend their time and energy on productive plants which they do not themselves own. Unemployment is a function of the labor group. The importance of recognizing this distinction becomes clearer when we consider the figures of unemployment. When we read an estimate of five or six million persons unemployed, our first tendency is to compare this number with the total population of one hundred and twenty-three million, and it does not seem so bad. But when we reflect that these are all wage-earners, and that there are only about twenty-eight million wage-earners in the country, the situation immediately takes on its true aspect of a prodigious calamity.

When, then, is a wage-earner unemployed? Certainly not during the hours outside the normal working day in his trade or occupation, even though he might personally like to work longer. Certainly not when he chooses to take a day or week off "on his own hook." Involuntariness is an essential factor in unemployment. But now the real difficulties begin to arise. Is a wage-earner unemployed if he is out on strike, especially if he has not personally voted for the strike? Or if his plant is experiencing a lock-out? Or if a strike in some related industry has forced a suspension of work in his plant? These are complicated and somewhat technical questions, but by no means devoid of practical bearings.

Much more important, however, is the matter of wages. Wages are the paramount economic factor in the life of a wage-earner. Employment is not employment to him except as it brings in wages. But how much wages? There is the rub. Wages in this country are not subject to even as much legal or conventional standardization as hours. Suppose, in a time like the present, a certain operative gives his force the choice between a complete shut-down of the plant or a cut of fifty per cent in wages. Suppose they refuse the cut—as workers often do—and are laid off. Are they unemployed? The *reductio ad absurdum* in this query, of course, is the question whether a worker is unemployed if there is a job available to him at one cent a day.

A definition of unemployment, then, must include considerations of a normal working force, normal hours, and normal wages. In a country like the United States, this means that it is impossible to frame an exact definition at all. But with these features in mind, it is possible to proceed to an intelligent and constructive consideration of the problem.

II

A person who would naturally be included in the normal wage-earning force of a society may find himself out of work for three main types of causes. First, he may be suffering from some mental or physical handicap which makes it unprofitable to employ him in any of the ordinary industries of the country—which, as we say, "unfits him to earn his living." Unemployment of this kind may be called "personal." Second, the activity in which he is engaged may be subject to fluctuation or interruptions at different periods of the year. This is "seasonal" unemployment. Third, his occupation may be affected by conditions which are inherent in the very structure of functioning of society itself. This is "societal" unemployment.

Personal unemployment has long been recognized, and there is an ancient assumption that most unemployment is of this kind. President Hadley, in his textbook on economics, says, "Among the many causes of 'unemployment' the two most important are the shiftlessness of individual laborers and the fluctuations of commercial credit." Similarly Dr. Antonio Stella, in his book "Some Aspects of Italian Immigration to the United States," makes the categorical statement, "There are always many people unemployed, especially in the slums of large cities, but those are the people who are either crippled or disabled or unwilling to work." In point of fact, personal unemployment is a very small part of the total, and with proper social administration could be reduced to almost negligible proportions. The popular impression on the subject is largely traceable to the fact that during a period of depression the persons who are conspicuously out of work are likely to have a decidedly decrepit or incompetent appearance (partly traceable, indeed, to the fact of unemployment). But during a brisk period, these very same individuals are given jobs and are actually sought out, thereby proving that they are not unemployable. But they are naturally the first to be laid off when bad times come. As someone has put it, "Personal qualities do not cause unemployment, but determine who shall be unemployed." We are told that in ancient Alexandria society was so well organized that even the blind and gouty were busy. If industry were really in need of labor it would be a poor specimen indeed who could not be fitted into the scheme of things. How insignificant a part of the grand total is represented by personal unemployment is revealed by the fact that practically all the figures of unemployment are based on those who have actually held jobs within a recent period.

Seasonal unemployment is of two main types. The first type arises in connection with those occupations which are directly dependent on the changing seasons of the year or on fashions that follow—or precede—the seasons. Agriculture is the most important, as well as the most easily understood, of these. In the temperate zones agricultural activities are positively controlled by the weather, particularly by temperature and rainfall. A worker whose sole occupation is tilling the soil finds the need of his services greatly reduced at certain seasons. This situation has been intensified by the introduction of machine methods and large-scale operation onto the farms. The odd jobs that used to keep the farmer busy during the winter months have now largely disappeared.

In general, the incidence of seasonal unemployment is greatest in the cold months, because the majority of productive occupations are unfavorably affected by extreme cold rather than heat. This is true not only of agriculture and most of the extractive industries, but also of construction enterprises, and outdoor work in general. On the other hand there are many occupations that have their busy season in the winter, such as lumbering, ice harvesting, gas manufacturing and coal mining.

The second type of seasonal unemployment appears in industries which are not directly affected by the climate, but by certain events fixed in the calendar. In this country the most notable example is Holiday Week. Candy and paper box manufacturers, department stores, and toy manufacturers, for example, have a very busy season preceding Christmas, and a decided slump afterwards.

Seasonal unemployment presents a much more serious problem than personal, and the numbers affected are much greater. But it is a simple and comprehensible phenomenon, and could be reduced to small proportions with relative ease if there were a really keen demand for labor, and a consequent incentive for society to apply its corporate intelligence to devising a genuinely efficient system of utilizing all the available labor.

III

It is societal unemployment that occasions the really serious distress and presents seriously baffling problems. As will be shown, it is basic not only to a full understanding of the other types, but also to any effective remedies for those types.

The central fact in societal unemployment is that about sixty per cent of the total gainfully employed population are wage-earners, who do not own the plant upon which they work. The fact of non-ownership is determinative. In our highly mechanized and capitalized economic system, certain prerogatives and powers go with the ownership of the physical plant. First of all, the owner of the physical plant—that is, the business as a going whole—owns the product. We hear a lot about labor getting "its share of the product." In point of fact, in any real sense, labor does not own any share of the product. Labor is paid by the owner of the product out of the proceeds of past products. Secondly, ownership of the plant carries with it management of the plant. The owner decides when the plant shall operate and when it shall shut down, what types of goods it shall turn out, how the productive processes shall be co-ordinated, and so on. Thirdly, with the ownership of the plant and of the product goes control of the disposition of the product. The owner determines selling prices, sales methods, rate of profits aimed at, and the redistribution of the proceeds for purposes of further production.

This factor of ownership is strangely ignored in the ordinary teaching of economics. Most conventional teachers of the subject still discourse about the four factors in production: Land, Labor, Capital, and Organization. They apparently fail to see that there has arisen a fifth factor, wholly distinct from any of the others. This fifth factor is Ownership, and it is unquestionably the characteristic and dominating feature of present-day production, and the one that causes the most acute and menacing social problems.

Having no part in the ownership of the business, nor of any portion of the material plant, labor's relation to the processes of production is merely that of an accessory. The labor class exerts no direct control over production. Its only control is through its influence on the market, that is, in its role as a consumer, not as a producer.

The extent to which the working class can affect the market depends entirely upon its purchasing power, and this in turn depends directly upon wages. From the labor point of view, accordingly, the typical situation can be summed up thus: Labor can affect the production of goods only as it offers a market for those goods; it can offer a market for goods only to the extent that it has purchasing power; it can have purchasing power only as it has wages; it can have wages only as it has employment; it can have employment only as the owners of businesses see fit to give it employment.

IV

This brings us to the other side of the situation. What is the characteristic attitude of the owners of businesses toward the employment of labor? Why, and under what conditions, do they wish to employ it? The sole reason why owners wish to employ labor, or are willing to employ it and pay it wages, is that without labor they cannot produce goods. The machines are domineering and mighty, but without at least a modicum of human labor they are impotent. Owners therefore find it necessary and desirable to employ human labor to the extent, and only to the extent, that it is indispensable in turning out the goods that they see fit to undertake to turn out. Anything that reduces the amount of labor required to turn out a given amount of goods will reduce their incentive to hire labor by just that amount.

Why, then, do owners wish to produce goods and what determines the amount and kinds of goods that they see fit to produce? The answer to these questions is found in just one word, which is the keyword to our whole economic system—*Profit*. Our entire economic mechanism is devised and manipulated exclusively for the purpose of profit. There is no use camouflaging it, and talking in smooth words about "Service" or "National Prosperity" or "American Industry". Any business that is a real business, and not pure philanthropy, which does not make profit not only will close, it *must* close. Any honest analysis of modern economic conditions must be willing to follow to the bitter end the quest for the nature, origin, and determination of profits.

"Profit" is one of the most misunderstood and mishandled of all the pet concepts in the befogged realm of conventional economics. It is usually described as the reward of organization. It is, in point of fact, the reward of ownership. Organization can be bought and paid for just like land, labor, and capital. If it chance that the owner himself provides the organization, he should charge the business with payment for it, just as he should charge the business for any land, labor, or capital that he himself may supply. Profits belong to the owner of the business, as owner exclusively. Profits consist in whatever is left over after all the other factors in production have received their compensation. This point can not be overstressed, for a grasp of it is vital to any true comprehension of the features of contemporary economic life.

Businesses, then, are conducted by their owners with an eye singly on profit. Profit depends upon the difference between the selling price of the product and the total cost of production. The wider the spread between these aggregates, the greater the profit. Inherently, therefore, the incentive of owners is to keep selling prices as high as possible and production costs as low as possible.

Now in the total cost of production, even with our highly mechanized industry, the wages of labor loom as a very large item. Probably nowhere in the whole complex of productive processes is so much pressure felt by owners to keep costs down as in the pay roll. Every saving or reduction in wages appears to them as so much clear gain.

And right here we put our finger on one of the basic contradictions, one of the central anomalies, that both create our social problems and make them so difficult of solution. The wage bill, which, looked at from one side, is an irritating item in the cost of production, to be reduced as low as possible, is, when viewed from the other side, an important and indispensable item in the purchasing power of the market which makes possible the realization of the hoped-for selling price, and which should therefore be kept as high as possible. Managers of businesses, in the existing economic system, are perpetually and inevitably fixed between this Scylla and Charybdis, and it is no wonder that they struggle and flounder helplessly and blindly a good deal of the time.

Naturally enough, the ordinary owner sees the cost aspect of wages most clearly. It is the nearest to him—often so close to his organ of vision as virtually to obscure the other aspect. The wages of his own force of workers are a direct and immediate charge on his business—they are only a remote and diffuse, often a completely indiscernible, factor in the market for his particular product. A manufacturer of steel rails can hardly visualize his workers as a part of the market for his product. Each producer, therefore, naturally strives to make what savings he can in his own wage bill, and leaves the effect on the sales of his products to chance or blind Fate. But in the aggregate, this individual distinction fades out, and the total wage-earning group becomes an important section of the total purchasing group—just one more case where the detached individual does not, and can hardly be expected to, see matters in their broad social implications.

V

The next query is, what are the features of the present social order that cause the labor force to be periodically or chronically in excess of the numbers required by business owners in their quest for profits?

The basic answer is found precisely in one of those truisms, the full meaning of which is seldom grasped just because of its familiarity: *Mechanization.*

As intimated above, the owners of businesses hire only so much labor as is necessary to produce the goods that will yield the maximum profits,—which does not by any means always mean the maximum possible quantity of goods. For this labor they pay the smallest amount necessary. If anything can be discovered that will be as effective as labor in producing goods, and that costs less, it will be substituted for labor. Such an agency is machinery. The economic history of the past century and a half is dominated by the progressive supplanting of labor by machinery in specific industries or occupations. The question of immediate interest in this connection is, what influence has this process had upon the demand for labor in the aggregate? The prevailing economic theory during this period has been that it did not diminish the total demand for labor, because the individual laborers displaced at each successive stage of the process quickly found employment in other fields, many of them opened up by the process of mechanization itself. Situations like the present seem to give the lie to this complacent philosophy. What are the facts?

The immediate effect of the introduction of mechanical factors into a new field is usually to reduce the direct cost of production. This may, or may not, be the prime reason for the step, but it is usually essential to the step. This means that a smaller amount of money is started on its circular course through the market to appear as purchasing power for the product. This would, in itself, tend to reduce the demand for the product, which in turn would tend toward a future reduction in the amount of product. Thus the circle is a vicious one, in the truest sense of the term. If the reduction in cost of production were accompanied by a corresponding reduction in selling price this would not be true. But there is no reason why this should be the case, and usually it is not. For the extra profits, which are the incentive for mechanization, depend upon an increase in the spread between costs and selling price, which would be lost if prices were reduced proportionally.

But the most important effect results from the difference between paying money for labor and paying it for machines. This difference is the fundamental factor in the whole situation. When money is paid for labor, it becomes purchasing power immediately, and purchasing power in the hands of those who have no other means of providing themselves with economic goods. Almost the entire amount, therefore, very quickly expresses itself in a demand for finished products.

The case is very different when the same amount of money is spent for machines, or more strictly, for the use of machines. Machines do not buy goods. This money passes beyond the machines—where? To other owners, the owners of the machines.

Now to a very large extent the owners of machines are the same people who own businesses. The effect of mechanization, therefore, is to shift purchasing power from the non-owning classes, who have no products to dispose of but only their labor, and to concentrate it in the hands of those who are owners of businesses, and accordingly have products to dispose of.

What effect has this on the total volume of the market for end products?

Clearly, the first effect is to reduce the number of *persons* in the market. The laborers who have lost their jobs and their wages, have also lost their purchasing power and are out of the picture. But has there been a corresponding reduction in the total *effective demand* of the market?

Here is precisely where one of the besetting fallacies of nineteenth century economics is revealed most clearly. The characteristic doctrine of this school in this department was that general overproduction is an impossibility. "Goods exchange for goods," and therefore no matter how many goods there may be there can never be an excess. The origin of this assumption is found in the damning error of the whole system—the inveterate tendency to think in terms of things instead of persons. Perhaps the classical economists should not be blamed too severely.

Knowing little or no psychology—there was none to be known—they had no clear understanding of how (not to say why) human beings behave. But since their whole (alleged) science rested on human behavior they had to invent a typical man, and endow him with a set of largely imaginary motives and modes of action. This famous economic man is a pathetic little puppet that bobs up and down, hither and thither, through the mazes of economic analysis, in response to strings pulled by a dominating interest in material things.

The truth is, not that "goods exchange for goods," but that persons who own goods do, or may, exchange them for goods owned by other persons. This is as far apart from the traditional assumption as the two poles. It removes the analysis from the realm of automatism, and places it in the realm of what is ordinarily called voluntary behavior. The question now becomes, how do the owners of goods actually feel toward the goods owned by other persons?

VI

Put this query in the form required by this present analysis—: Granting that the same amount of product is turned out after an extensive process of mechanization as before, but that the purchasing power is now concentrated in a smaller and wealthier section of the population, will the total demand for goods be as great as before?

If one of the other basic assumptions of traditional economics were true, the answer would be, Yes. This is the assumption that human desires are infinite, and it is fundamentally false. (No animosity, please understand, against conventional economists. But they have a heavy responsibility for the present situation, and must be prepared to face the music.) Looking into the infinite future, it might be possible to say that human desires are infinite. But at any given time, with respect to the types of goods that actually exist at that time, they are strictly limited. Any intelligent person can demonstrate this to himself. Let him imagine himself endowed with infinite purchasing power, and then let him ask himself how many grand pianos he would wish, or how many mansions, or how many steam yachts, automobiles or airplanes. He would realize that his desires for any and all of these things are strictly limited. Then let him descend to more prosaic matters, and ask himself how many suits of clothes, or pairs of shoes, or pounds of beefsteak, or theatre tickets, or golf balls he would buy in a year. By a simple process of self-examination it becomes clear that the total potential demand of any individual for all the types of material things that exist at any given time is a definitely limited quantity.

If this is true of every individual, it is true of society. The reason why it seems untrue is that so large a proportion of the population have incomes far inferior to their desires that the total unfilled demand of society seems infinite. If attention is centered on the possessors of vast incomes it is easy to realize that their unsatisfied desire for enjoyable goods approaches, if it does not actually reach, zero. J. J. Astor is reported to have said, "I can do nothing with my income but buy more land, build more houses, and lend money on mortgages." This, it will be noted, means investing instead of spending, the significance of which will be touched on shortly.

The general principle that emerges from this analysis is: *The smaller the number of individuals in whose hands a given amount of income is concentrated, the smaller will be the effective demand for consumable goods represented by that income.* If another *reductio ad absurdum* is needed to make this clear, it can be furnished by imagining that the total year's product of the economic plant of the United States were equally divided between two owners. To what extent would "goods exchange for goods"?

This is the fatal quality of mechanization under private ownership. It tends to concentrate purchasing power more and more in the hands of those who already have an excess above their personal demands, and to remove it from those whose desires are far in excess of their purchasing power. The profit motive drives owners to divert income from the very channels which make profits possible. Business owners can be counted on to buy part of each other's product, but they will not buy it all, and the richer individually the owners are the smaller the proportion of the product that will be bought.

Instead of buying end products with all his income, the large income receiver invests a large portion of it. But investing simply means creating more machines, and a more capacious productive plant, thereby enlarging the volume of goods to be produced, while decreasing the proportionate demand for them.

Thus, looked at from any angle, the system is revealed as inherently self-destructive. The search for profits first of all works deprivation on those who do not share in profits, and eventually, through them, destroys the very conditions which make profits possible.

If the question is raised why, if this is true, western society has not gone on the rocks long ago, the answer is furnished by reflecting that the features of a transition period are quite different from those of the period when the new factors are thoroughly established and fully operative. The classical economists wrote in the presence of the phenomena of a transition period. They saw those phenomena, and could hardly be expected to see anything else. Naturally they made the mistake of considering them permanent, and so wrote into their system as eternal "economic laws" generalizations which were essentially temporary and ephemeral in their validity. Today the transition period is rapidly coming to a close, and the permanent features of a mechanized society are confronting us in all their stark ugliness and horror. Unemployment is only one, though a dominant one, of these features.

VII

What of the remedies?

As indicated above, chronic unemployment, a permanent and increasing excess of labor over the needs of the present economic system, is the basic factor in the whole situation. So-called cyclical unemployment is merely a special temporary aggravation of the permanent situation, originating in the speculative element in most modern business, with its long-time processes, and its production for an anticipated and uncertain future market. These forces and their operation have been so thoroughly and familiarly expounded in the various treatises on the business cycle that they need no elaboration here.

Until chronic unemployment can be eliminated, there is little hope of relieving either cyclical unemployment, or the two forms first mentioned, personal and seasonal. Remedies for these two are well known, simple, and easy to understand. But they are either useless from the social point of view, or actually worse than the disease.

Consider first of all personal unemployment. Since this is due to defects of the individual, it would seem to be curable by the removal of these defects. From the individual point of view this is true. But socially there is no gain whatever. For as long as there is a permanent reservoir of unemployed, due to an excess of available labor over the actual total demand, the improvement of any individual's efficiency will not diminish the total volume of unemployment. His increased efficiency will not add to the total demand for labor, but will simply result in some other worker's losing the job that he gets. In fact, under existing conditions, this process of increasing industrial efficiency is inherently injurious to labor as a class. For the higher the level of efficiency among workers in general, the smaller will be the labor force required to turn out a given product, and hence the greater the proportion of unemployed.

The same principles hold for seasonal unemployment. Methods of dealing with this evil through "dovetailing," better planned and better balanced production, etc., are well known, and their efficacy on an individual basis has been demonstrated. But no matter how widely they might be applied there would be no alleviation of the social situation. For if Mary Jones, a fur worker, who has habitually been out of a job about half the year, learns the artificial flower trade, and Bessie Smith, a flower worker, learns the fur trade, it does not add to the total demand for either fur or flower workers. If any change at all takes place, it simply means that Mary is employed the whole year and Bessie not at all, or vice versa. Much the same situation exists with respect to unemployment bureaus and all forms of personally remedial agencies.

Unemployment is a striking example of a type of social evil, familiar to all students of group relations, where the natural personal remedy is no social remedy at all. It is like giving a concert that will attract twelve hundred persons, in a hall that will seat only one thousand. The logical expedient, for you and me as individuals, is obviously to go early. But no matter how many individuals adopt this remedy, the total situation remains unimproved. In fact, the more who adopt it, the greater is the confusion and loss of time, and still two hundred will have to stand or go home. There are only two real remedies—either to hire a larger hall or a poorer singer.

VIII

The only effective remedies for unemployment of any kind or all kinds must be thorough-going modifications in the structure or functioning of society itself. There is one outstanding remedy that emerges logically and irresistibly from an honest analysis of the situation and the factors involved. This is the common ownership of the entire productive plant by all the workers, or by society itself. This might, or might not, involve the distribution of the product on an even per capita basis among all the workers of every grade. But at any rate, it would result in a much evener and more equable distribution than at present, and consequently a healthier economic condition. The opportunity to work of certain individuals would not then be dependent on the will of other individuals, personal or corporate. The profit motive would disappear, and production could be carried on on a basis of social utility instead of personal gain. The entire mechanism could be intelligently co-ordinated, and the total productive effort distributed and directed in such a way as to promote the greatest happiness of the group as a whole.

It needs no great familiarity with revolutionary social thought to recognize in this expedient the hallmark of socialism. But what of it? Let us at least be logical. Let us be honest. Let us be willing to follow a systematic analysis to its inevitable conclusion, and then see what action is indicated. Granted that there is no authoritative socialist doctrine today that offers a workable scheme for putting this principle into practice. Granted that there are many and difficult obstacles in the way of making the necessary practical adjustments. All this is no excuse for shutting our eyes to the facts, and refusing to apply our intelligence to the determination of the next steps, starting at any point to which the pursuit of truth may have brought us. The individualistic-capitalistic system has proved itself incapable thus far of coping with the problem. Socialism at least presents a concrete idea. If any one has a better solution, let him offer it. Nothing could be worse than the present confusion—except the future calamity that is surely impending unless some genuinely constructive remedies are found and adopted, and that right soon.

8

STATISTICS V. COMMON SENSE

Written in 1915

BAGEHOT'S FAMOUS impressive, if unconventional, statement of his mistrust of statistics† has lately been gaining new warrant. The reformers of to-day are thoroughly addicted to the statistical method, and have made figures a twentieth century fetish, subject to all the abuses and superstitions which surround fetishes. This makes the activities of twentieth century agitators much more dangerous than those of an earlier day.

The author of "Social Untruth and the Social Unrest" in the April, 1914, number of THE UNPOPULAR REVIEW put his finger on a very sore spot in our social organization. If would-be reformers could once be persuaded that they injure, each his own cause, and all the causes of improvement in general, by the attempt to bolster up their schemes by ill-considered and false accusations and charges, they would certainly devote more time to verification and less to vociferation. There are countless broad-minded and sympathetic citizens who

[† "Lies, damned lies, and statistics".]

look with suspicion or derision on the whole of what they term the "uplift crowd" simply because of the inexcusably careless and often dishonest methods by which they work. The distinctions between these modern reform movements and the efforts of Dickens in "Nicholas Nickleby" are well brought out by this writer.

It would be interesting to study out just why an array of figures carries such a convincing weight of authority to the average individual. Probably the basic reason is that in many cases the most scientific of demonstrations take the form of statistical tables, and that only in this way can many propositions be proved. But whatever the causes, the fact is that anyone who presents his arguments in the form of tables, and his conclusions in dogmatic statements presumably based on the tables, is sure to convince nine-tenths of his readers. The very complexity and mystery of the tabulations has the same stimulating effect on the credulity of the observer that the grotesque accoutrements of the primitive medicine man have upon the mind of the savage. The oracular pronouncements in either case are accepted on the basis of an uncomprehended but imposing authority.

This characteristic of the statistical method gives rise to three separate forms of abuse. The first two lie with the propounders of the statistics, the third with the recipient. In the first place, honest and well-meaning, but untrained, agitators use their statistics in the sincere conviction that they do actually prove the propositions advanced, when a little accurate analysis would often show them fallacious. Secondly, skillful statisticians, either seeking unworthy ends, or obsessed with the belief that a worthy end justifies an unworthy means, sometimes juggle statistics. It is not always possible for anyone except the author himself to decide in which of these two classes certain productions ought to be placed. The third form of abuse is simply the credulous acceptance and requotation, by the general public, of any set of propositions or assertions which appears to emanate from a statistical investigation.

There is also, of course, an opposite type of mind, represented by the man who says: "You can prove anything by statistics," and consequently declines to accept any statistical demonstration whatever. Such was a certain friend of the present writer, when the subject under discussion was whether wage scales had gone up or down in the United States in recent years. The writer started for a book-case to consult a few volumes on economics, but his friend hastily interrupted him, saying, "No, no! Don't show me any figures. I take no stock in figures." The argument terminated abruptly. But this type of person is rather uncommon, and whatever other pitfalls he may be liable to, he is at least free from the dangers which arise from the unquestioning acceptance of statistics.

Still another feature of modern social untruths, is that in many cases the truth is often a matter of expert knowledge, the general public must rely upon a very small group of authorities and if the expert opinion is rendered in a statistical way, any adequate criticism involves an investigation virtually as difficult as that upon which the report is based. Statistics on social questions all too frequently circulate solely on the assumed reliability of the authority who propounds them: The general public has not time nor inclination to examine credentials very judiclally.

There is, however, also a very large group of misleading statistics for the detection of which no expert knowledge is required. A slight application of that rare and invaluable article known as common sense will suffice. To mistakes of this kind, strange as it may seem, the professional statistician seems particularly susceptible. There appears to be something connected with the constant use of figures, which tends to inhibit the power of considering phenomena in any other than numerical terms, or of judging of them by any other than the mathematical faculties.

A few examples may not be uninteresting.

At an informal dinner one of the guests spoke of the seriousness of cancer, and remarked that statistics showed it to be a greater cause of death in the United States than tuberculosis. The writer protested, with more vehemence, it is to be feared, than courtesy, that such a thing was impossible. "Oh, no, it isn't," was the reply, "I read it in a medical journal." The question was dropped, and the writer was left to wonder whether it was a case of misreading an accurate article, or publication of absurd statistics in a supposedly reliable organ. That it was the latter was revealed by the receipt, a few days later, of an editorial from the New York Evening Post, which read in part as follows:

> That is an amazing error which somehow found its way into the columns of the Medical Record, in an editorial on cancer reprinted in the Times of Sunday. "In 1910," says the Record, "there were 12,557 more deaths from cancer than from tuberculosis in the registration area, thereby showing the greater importance of cancer over tuberculosis, and the great need of education in the knowledge of the disease."

The Post editorial then cites figures showing that, in

fact, the deaths from cancer were less by 45,000 than those from tuberculosis, and then proceeds:

> The error was doubtless due to some accidental interchange of figures; but it is difficult to understand how anyone deeply interested in such a subject could be thus misled. The occurrence may serve as a reminder of the constant need, in using statistics, of the check supplied by those inaccurate but broadly trustworthy data which are indicated by common knowledge; or, as the case may be, by a priori considerations. This check has more frequently to be applied to the drawing of inferences than to the citation of the primary figures; but indeed there is no direction in which one can afford to be off his guard.

Here, then, is a striking example of the typical career of a set of figures which ignore facts known to the veriest school-boy. Started by some careless tabulator (it is impossible to conceive of any adequate motive for intentional misrepresentation) they are made the basis of an editorial discussion by a supposed expert, reprinted in a reliable daily, and quoted in ordinary conversation by no one knows how many laymen. Mistakes of this particular kind, however, are comparatively innocuous. In this case, they could hardly affect the death rate from either disease, and any attention drawn temporarily to cancer as a result of this exaggeration would be likely to do more good than harm.

An example of utterly meaningless, to say nothing of inaccurate, statistics is that referred to in an indignant letter to the New York Times, printed on November 18, 1913. The opening paragraph was:

> In the window of the headquarters of a woman

> suffrage organization is a placard reading: "Are you aware that a baby dies every eleven seconds throughout the civilized world?" As nothing is added, it seemingly implicates the anti-suffrage people of both sexes in the gentle art of murder or neglectfulness of the young. I plead not guilty; nor do I entertain the most remote suspicion of any acquaintance so addicted.

The writer of the letter not only objected to the implication of these figures, but also pertinently pointed out that the "exact figures of infant mortality are simply unprocurable." The most amusing feature of all, however, in connection with this statement is the very efficient defense secured to the author by leaving a margin of safety of at least four or five hundred per cent through the use of the somewhat vague and indefinite term "baby." If his (or her) figures were proved too large for children under one year of age, it could easily be replied that they were meant to include all under two, or three, or five, as circumstances might require.

Whether because of the semi-sacred character of death, or because it is closely allied with the supernatural, the whole question of death rates seems to be specially set apart from the application of common sense tests. A recent case in point is cited in The Nation for January 7, 1915. "The National Wholesale Liquor Dealers of America find no trouble in disposing of the ridiculous assertion made by Mr. Hobson in the Prohibition debate, that 'Alcohol averages 2,000 American lives a day; alcohol actually kills fully 730,000 citizens every year.' On the basis of the United States Census mortality statistics, it is figured out that the total number of deaths of persons over five years of age in the United States, from all causes, is about 2,500 a day, so that, if we exclude children under five, Mr. Hobson's statement would leave only 500 deaths to occur daily from all other causes, as against the 2,000 due to alcohol." The reader is left to query whether the liquor dealers have not made just as foolish an error as Mr. Hobson, in arbitrarily omitting children under five. The deaths in this age group number nearly one-quarter of the total. Why should they be omitted in reckoning the deaths due to alcohol? The only logical reason for so doing would be that none of them was attributable to alcohol. Did the liquor dealers mean to imply that this was the case? It requires no special generosity to Mr. Hobson to presume that in speaking of the devastation of alcohol he meant to include—as was perfectly legitimate—the indirect as well as the direct effects of the drug. Any one who knows anything about infant mortality knows that a very large percentage of it is traceable to the effects of alcohol. It is one of the great racial poisons, because of its effect on the germ cell and embryo. If the shades of all the children under five whose brief career is terminated each year by the ills traceable to alcoholic parents—prenatal injury, malnutrition, improper feeding, cruelty, abuse, and neglect of every sort—they would present an emphatic protest against being omitted when the indictment is drawn up against alcohol.

Incidentally it is worth mentioning that the figures given in the above quotation are themselves open to question. The total number of deaths in the registration area, representing 63.2 per cent of the total population, was 838,251 in 1912; that of children under five was 204,-639. For the entire country this figures out over 3,600 deaths per day altogether, and over 2,700 omitting children under five. Allowing for two years' growth of population this would bring the total number of deaths up toward 4,000. So that the deaths attributed by Mr. Hobson to alcohol would amount to nearer one-half of the total than the four-fifths mentioned in the context of the passage quoted. All this does not justify Mr. Hobson's statement. But the blackness of the pot detracts very decidedly from the force of what it has to say about the kettle.

In the United States the question of immigration, complicated as it is—entangled with every department of national life, subject to all sorts of prejudices and preconceived notions—furnishes many notable examples of absurd statistics. Such cases as the comparison of the "old" and the "new" immigration with reference to pauperism, without taking into consideration the respective length of residence in the United States of each group; or comparing the criminality of native-born and foreign-born without corrections for sex and age; or comparing the earnings of the modern immigrant with those of the immigrant of half a century ago, in terms of dollars and cents, without correction for the increased cost of living —such as these are too frequent and too prominent to need specific citation. Many others, of only slightly less obvious absurdity, occur in many of the supposedly scientific writings on the subject. A couple of illustrations may suffice.

Dr. Peter Roberts, in his book "The New Immigration", page 49, says: "The new immigration in one respect differs very markedly from the old; the percentage of farmers and farm laborers in this new stream is sixfold what it was in the old." This assertion is sufficiently startling to challenge the attention of anyone who has devoted the least study to questions of immigration. But that its inclusion in this book is not due to mere inadvertence is shown by the fact that a footnote elaborates it, and refers to a table in the appendix on which it is supposed to rest. This table is taken from the report of the Immigration Commission, and shows the previous occupations of the foreign-born male employees *now employed* in the *manufacturing* and *mining industries* of the United States. It tells nothing about the characteristics of various races as a whole, and certainly nothing about the old immigration when it was at its height. But this is not all. In order to make the comparison more striking, the author omits the Irish from the count in the case of the old immigration, and the Hebrews from the new immigration, because the facts with reference to these races are in contradiction to the statement made. But to omit the Irish is to omit a third or so of one of the groups compared, while to omit the Hebrews is to leave out a very considerable fraction of the other. Then, to cap the climax, in order to get the averages, the author adds up the percentages of farmers in each race, and divides the total by the number of races, without paying any attention to their respective numerical importance in the immigration stream. Thus the Welsh, with a percentage of farmers amounting to 2.6 have the same importance in determining the average as the Germans with a percentage of farmers of 28.8, although the former race was numerically an almost negligible factor, in the total current of the old immigration.

This was a case where the complete criticism of the statistics is somewhat complicated, and involves some acquaintance with the sources of information, as well as some slight knowledge of the rudiments of statistical science. The role of common sense in such a case is merely to wave the red flag, and warn writer and reader alike that there must be something wrong with figures which seem to establish a conclusion so entirely contrary to common knowledge.

Another book on immigration which has attracted a large amount of attention is Dr. Hourwich's "Immigration and Labor." This volume illustrates in an extraordinary way the possibilities and the dangers of the statistical method in popularizing notions about social questions. The author, ostensibly for the sake of the "busy reader," embodies his conclusions in a preliminary chapter, called a "Summary Review," assuring the readers, busy and other, that for each proposition here advanced there is a demonstration somewhere in the vast accumulation of statistical matter which follows. In reading the reviews of this book it is amusing and significant to note the facility and unanimity with which the reviewers circumnavigate this compact mass of statistics, either avoiding responsibility by a vague reference to the thought-provoking and erudite compilation of figures, or else following the author's lead, and accepting the weight of the figures as proof of the conclusions. A case in point is an editorial in the New York Times, which, with some apparent awe, refers to the author as a man who has "gone to the record," the evident assumption being that his conclusions must therefore be accurate.

This book is, in fact, an example of the sort of production which cannot possibly be adequately criticized by anyone who has not devoted years of study to the subject, and who is not well versed in the statistical method. At the same time, all through the "Summary Review," there are countless statements and arguments which ought to challenge the common sense of any intelligent reader, and would, if that faculty were not narcotized by the influence of the statistics in the rest of the book. A sufficient example is furnished by the following two sentences, which contain, in a sense, the thesis of the whole book. They fall under numbers one and four in a series of six brief statements which sum up the preliminary chapter.

> Recent immigration has displaced none of the native American wage-earners or of the earlier immigrants, but has only covered the shortage of labor resulting from the excess of the demand over the supply.
>
> Recent immigration has not reduced the rates of wages, nor has it prevented an increase in the rate of wages.

This is an extraordinary instance of audacious confidence in the paralyzing effect of statistics on common sense. Anyone who has ever looked inside the covers of an economic textbook ought to recognize at a glance the dubious character of an argument which assumes to show that a certain phenomenon has supplied a shortage of labor without preventing a rise in the wages of labor which would otherwise have occurred. By which one of the many theories of wages can one support the assertion that something which neutralizes an excess of demand over supply does not block a rise in wages? Yet, apparently, these two mutually contradictory statements have "got by" with many readers and reviewers.

A simple case of the sort of statistical legerdemain by which Dr. Hourwich's general statements are supported is found in the author's discussion of the question of child labor. In order to prove that the foreign-born are no more inclined to send their children into factories than the native-born, he compares the percentages of working children of native and foreign parentage with the percentages of all native-born and foreign-born persons in the entire group employed in manufactures. Finding that these two sets of percentages are nearly identical, he considers his point proved. But the briefest consideration shows that this comparison has no logic whatever back of it. The legitimate comparison is the percentage of the total number of children of foreign parentage who are now employed, with the percentage of the total number of children of native parentage who are employed. Figures for this comparison are readily accessible in the same sources from which the author drew his data. They show that in fact the percentage of children of foreign parentage who are at work is nearly three times that of the children of native parentage. Obviously, the fallacy lies in ignoring the fact that a much smaller proportion of the total population of foreign parentage are children, than of the population of native parentage.

Errors and misstatements of the sort just discussed are full of danger and sure to do harm. Immigration is one of a number of important and serious public problems now before the American people. In the safe handling and proper solution of such questions in a democracy, the one thing most needed is a wide dissemination of accurate knowledge. Since almost everybody is dependent for his facts on a very small body of investigators and students, incalculable injury is bound to result if these supposed authorities send out misleading and erroneous—not to say false—data, disguised in the cloak of a statistical investigation.

But there is another set of social problems where

false statistics do even more harm than in the case of those of which immigration is typical. This is especially true if the misstatements take the form particularly referred to by the author of "Social Untruth and Social Unrest"—that of exaggeration. These are problems of a distinctly moral nature, where one of the chief checks to their spread lies in the belief that they are discountenanced by the great mass of the members of one's social group. Foremost among these are the various sexual evils. One of the greatest barriers to the extension of prostitution and its kindred evils is the belief that they are condemned in theory and scorned in practice by the best members of society, while conversely one of the surest means of increasing their dominion is to spread the conviction that their practice is well-nigh universal. The lure of the average is so great that most men are content to be no better than the great majority. And anything which tends to lower the popular conception of the morality of the majority, tends also to degrade the personal standards of individuals.

In spite of these facts, not only the sensation-mongers, but many sincere workers for reform, seem to be possessed by an irresistible impulse to paint the situation in the darkest possible colors, not only as regards its character but as regards its extent. Some of these statements are very difficult to check up. One such occurs in Act III of "Damaged Goods" where the doctor voices his estimate that all but four men out of a thousand have exposed themselves to venereal contamination. This may possibly be an accurate statement for Paris or for France. It is surely very doubtful if it comes anywhere near the truth for the United States. At least, nobody knows with certainty. And until we do know, nothing but harm can result from the wide circulation of an estimate which common knowledge would mark as far above the limit of probability.

Other statements tending in the same direction are fortunately more susceptible of accurate checking up. An example of this sort of statistics, and of the method of verifying them, is presented in an old book on Magdalenism, written by Rev. Ralph Wardlaw in 1843. Discussing the estimates of the prevalence of prostitution which were current in his day, he selects for examination the statement that there were 80,000 prostitutes in London. He then notes the common saying, which apparently obtained as much credence then as now, that the average life of such a woman, after entering the career, is five years. But in order to err on the safe side, he assumes it to be ten years, making a death rate for this class of one in ten, or 8,000 annually in London. The next step is to compare this number of deaths of prostitutes with the total number of deaths of women in London, with the startling result that in the year July 1, 1838 to June 30, 1839, every female who died between the ages of fifteen and fifty must have been a prostitute, and that 2,014 more must have been taken from the age group between fifty and sixty-five to make up the required 8,000. Not a single virtuous female could have died between the ages of fifteen and fifty.

It might seem at first thought that statistics of this sort must be an affair of a much earlier generation than the present, and that such an unsupportable estimate could not possibly find currency in the twentieth century. Yet it is necessary to go back only half a decade to find a statement of an almost identical character, emanating from a source which would tend to give it much weight.

The source is Dr. Charles E. Woodruff's book, "Expansion of Races," and the statement is found on page 193, where the author accepts the estimate that there must be nearly 1,000,000 prostitutes in the United States, and goes on to compute that since they live on the average only five years, there must be 200,000 deaths of prostitutes every year.

There are several methods of testing this statement. In the first place, since most prostitutes are between the ages of fifteen and thirty-nine, and since the total number of women in these age groups in the United States in 1910 was 19,293,171, it would mean that one out of every nineteen women between fifteen and thirty-nine must be a prostitute. Now it takes twenty-five years to replace the population in the age groups from fifteen to thirty-nine. But the group of prostitutes must be replaced every five years. That is, from the entire group of girls reaching a certain age each year, enough must be devoted to a life of prostitution to provide for 200,000 deaths from that class. There are, in round numbers, about 1,000,000 girls (making due allowance for immigrants) who reach the age of fifteen each year. Therefore, to keep the ranks of unfortunate women full, approximately one out of every five girls reaching the age of fifteen would have to enter a life of prostitution.

The foregoing conclusions, while they outrage common sense on the face of them, do not *prove* the falsity of the estimate in question. The best, clearest, and most convincing proof is obtained by adopting exactly the method of Mr. Wardlaw. According to the mortality statistics of the Census Bureau, the total number of deaths of females between fifteen and thirty-nine in the registration area, in the year 1909, was 62,659. The estimated population of the registration area in that year was 50,870,518, while the estimated population of continental United States was 90,556,521. If the deaths of females bore the same proportion to total population in the entire country as in the registration area—and there could not be any wide discrepancy—the total number of deaths of females between fifteen and thirty-nine would be 113,532—hardly more than half the number claimed by Dr. Woodruff for prostitutes alone.

The same author quotes from a medical journal an estimate that in New York City there are from 40,000 to 50,000 public prostitutes, the majority of them being from fifteen to twenty-five years old, and the average duration of the life of abandonment being four years. This would mean at least 10,000 deaths of prostitutes per year in New York City. The reference for this estimate is carelessly quoted, and cannot be verified, so that for New York City it will be better to refer to a more recent, and possibly more moderate, estimate, made by a government investigator, and blazoned in headlines in the New York Times for January 30, 1913. (The fact that a later report denied that this person was a government investigator simply emphasizes the carelessness of the whole proceeding.) This authority puts the number of white slaves—not to mention other prostitutes—in New York City at 26,000 at the beginning of the year 1913. The total number of deaths in New York City in the year 1912, between the ages of ten and twenty-nine (the nearest available age grouping) was 8,092. Not more than half of these could have been females. (The number of deaths in the registration cities in these age groups is considerably greater for males than for females.) That is, there would have been not more than 4,046 deaths of females between the ages of ten and twenty-nine in the year in question. If the entire number were prostitutes, it would not be nearly enough to make up the required number of deaths for the 26,000 white slaves alone, at the rate of one death in five.

There is no need to cite farther illustrations or to elaborate the question at length. The point is clear. Statistics are a most valuable and indispensable instrument in the study of social questions. Many truths can be arrived at only by their use. But like many keen and efficient tools, they are most dangerous in the hands of unskilled, unscrupulous, or reckless manipulators. Intentionally or unintentionally they may be made to defeat their own true purpose, becoming the means of disseminating conjecture instead of fact, falsehood in the place of truth. They need to be continually tested, by writer and reader alike, by every other means which can be brought to bear on the question under consideration. So insidious are the dangers, that the mere appearance of a statistical table ought to be a signal for the marshalling of every element of care and caution which can be summoned. A statistical table is not, in itself, a demonstration of a truth. Nor, on the other hand, is nothing true which cannot be proved by statistics. Statistics are good. But they must not be allowed to take the place of logic, observation, and common sense. And the greatest of these is common sense.

9

HUNGER V. LOVE

Written in 1926

I

IN THE churches of Sweden, Tylor tells us, there used to be kept certain clumsy wooden clubs, some of which have been preserved as objects of curiosity down to the present day. They were called "family clubs" and they were used to terminate the existence of persons who had grown aged or hopelessly ill. The agents of this solemn procedure were the near relatives of those about to die; presumably, as a rule their children or grand-children. This is only one instance of a custom, widely followed by savage peoples, and others not so savage, whereby the younger generation ceremonially and conventionally eliminates those of its elders who can no longer do their part in a struggle for existence always arduous and precarious. The method differs in different countries. Among many roving tribes, with whom life depends upon movement, an undue consideration of the old would involve the sacrifice of the entire group. Those who can no longer keep the pace are made as comfortable as possible with a little fire, a few scraps of food, and perhaps a rude shelter, and then left to their fate. In other cases the methods are more violent, not infrequently involving cannibalism in some form. William G. Sumner, in his "Folkways," gives page after page of examples of this custom in its diverse manifestations.

In some instances the old people protest and plead for delay; in others they recognize the procedure as necessary and appropriate, urge on the executioners to do their duty, and even demand the lethal stroke as a right. Explanations of the procedure differ among different peoples. In some cases there is a frank recognition that it is due to the necessity of conserving the food supply, and promoting the economic and military efficiency of the group. In other cases the alleged purpose is to spare the aged a long period of suffering, or at least a joyless existence when they can no longer indulge in the hunt, the dance, or the feast. Sometimes there is a belief that only those who die a violent death are assured of the full blessings of the after life. It is probable that in practically all cases the first explanation expresses the actual evolutionary basis of the custom, and that the kindlier interpretations are in the nature of "rationalizations."

As an increasing mastery over nature enabled man to enter, in some degree at least, upon a surplus economy, the practice was gradually abandoned. Yet it lingered on even in Europe to a surprisingly late date, doubtless being perpetuated by the force of tradition after its economic justification had disappeared. Thus Tylor in his "Anthropology" says, "The Wends in what is now Germany practiced the hideous rite of putting the aged and infirm to death, cooking and eating them, much as Herodotus describes the old Massagetae as doing." Furthermore, even among highly civilized peoples a resort to the primitive expedient is not unknown in times of extreme stress. "Colonel Fremont, in 1849, in a letter to his wife, tells how in crossing the plains he and his comrades left the weak and dying members of their party, one by one, to die in the snow, after lighting a little fire for him." The ceremonial or religious character in which these practices are customarily enveloped undoubtedly represents an expedient worked out by the group to guarantee that the killing shall be a fully sanctioned societal measure, safeguarded as far as possible from arbitrary employment to promote the selfish interests of the individual relatives.

Widespread as is this custom of the killing of the old by the young, it would undoubtedly be much more common and much more familiar to us were it not that the converse practice—the killing of the young by the old, of children by parents—is vastly more common. The reason for this is perfectly simple; the elders get the first chance. Long before the new member of the group has developed wit enough to comprehend the competitive nature of the existence into which he has been introduced, or force enough to do anything about it, those already in command of the situation have had ample opportunity to consider what bearing an additional individual will have upon their personal or group welfare, and to act accordingly. This decision may be made and put into effect at almost any stage in the child's development. Very frequently this is done during the pre-natal period. Abortion is by no means confined to civilized peoples, but is hoary with antiquity, and is employed by groups on almost every stage of cultural evolution. The painful and dangerous character of the means employed among many primitive tribes testifies to the strength of the desire to prevent the appearance of a new claimant to the limited supplies of the family or the group.

Much more conspicuous than abortion—whether more prevalent or not it would be difficult to say—is infanticide. The social usages governing this practice are indescribable in their multiplicity among peoples in every quarter of the globe and on every stage of cultural evolution. Aside from the extra-conventional killing of infants by their parents which even the most prosperous and advanced societies have not been able wholly to eliminate, there is a vast amount of infanticide which accords with recognized standards and enjoys complete social sanction. Not infrequently this sanction expresses itself in ritual, but there does not seem to be the same degree of ceremonial flavor about this custom that there is about the killing of the old—perhaps just because it is too commonplace.

Here, too, a variety of explanations is alleged for both abortion and infanticide. The former may be due to reluctance to undergo the pain of bearing children and the trouble of rearing them, to fear of lacerations, or injury to the figure, to a desire to "spite the husband," and to a candid fear that the food supply may be insufficient. Infanticide may be explained on the ground of defects or weaknesses on the part of the children—as among the Spartans, whose practice of it Aristotle approved—or by the difficulty a mother experiences under primitive conditions of caring for two small infants at once; or by various arbitrary conventions of propriety, such as the notion that a woman should not have a second child until the first is ten years old, that it is discreditable to have a child within the first two or three years of marriage, or that it is shameful to have children unevenly divided between the sexes. In almost all cases, however, it is probably safe to assume that the underlying motive of infanticide is a more or less subconscious recognition of the necessity of limiting the competition of life by restraining the growth of population. Support is given to this interpretation by the much greater prevalence of female, than of male or general, infanticide.

In some cases the unwillingness to bring children into the world reaches the point where it actually threatens "race suicide." Not enough children are born, or at least allowed to live, to keep up the number of the group. At least one tribe has been reported where no children at all are born (except occasionally by accident), the population being maintained by buying children from the neighboring tribes. The wide diffusion and virtual universality of these various practices would seem to argue that they arise out of some deep-seated general characteristics of human individuals or human societies, or perhaps that they trace back of human origins and are representatives of all living organisms, a natural concomitant of all life itself. Further inquiry lends assurance to the latter conclusion.

II

The central fact of conflict in Nature—commonly designated as the "struggle for existence"—is now a commonplace, and needs no emphasis. It is not, however, always recognized how generally this struggle expresses itself in killing.

> To him who, in the love of Nature, holds
> Communion with her visible forms

there comes in time the startling realization that one of her most characteristic aspects is that of a gigantic slaughterhouse. A large part of the processes of Nature consists in great cycles of slaying. The hawk kills the sparrow, the sparrow kills the worm, the worm kills the tree, the tree kills the shrub, the shrub kills the grass, the grass kills the wild strawberry, and so on and on and on. This killing divides itself into two distinct types. First, the active, aggressive killing that is associated with pursuit, attack, capture, and quick destruction. Second, the passive, persistent killing that results from success in the competition for the limited supplies of nature. The second of these forms is universal to all living organisms, the first is virtually restricted to animals, the difference being that plants get their subsistence, as a rule from the soil, which (fortunately) can not be killed since it is not alive, while animals derive their sustenance from other living creatures, plants or animals.

Obviously, therefore, the passive form of slaughter is vastly more important, and accounts for an immeasurably larger number of deaths, the world over, than the active form. The competition of life is keenest between those organisms which are most alike, and which therefore make the most nearly identical demands upon nature. There is no competition between the codfish and the song-sparrow; but there is active competition between the song-sparrow and the purple finch because both depend upon seeds. This competition accordingly becomes keenest of all between members of the same species, and reaches its climax when they are attempting to subsist in the same area. This is another way of saying that in all this bitter competition in nature, the most relentless struggle is that between parents and children.

Consider, for example, the case of the pine tree. A six year old naturalist, walking through the pine woods with her father, propounded the query, "Daddy, where are all the baby trees?" There were, in point of fact, no baby trees, or none to speak of. There never are baby trees in pine forests. Yet the pine trees are always bringing offspring into the world, hundreds of thousands, millions, of them every year. But with almost negligible exceptions they all die, and the agents of their destruction are the elder generation who have already pre-empted the place in the sun. Only here and there does a fortunate scion manage to find an unoccupied crevice where it can get a root-hold and enough light and air to permit it to grow. Those who do, and who eventually develop into sturdy saplings, have their revenge by becoming the means whereby the more senile and decrepit of their elders receive their final death blow.

So it is with all trees. They are liberal enough in bringing young into the world, but they are absolutely relentless in refusing them an opportunity to survive in the parental neighborhood. The only way for the youthful tree to see life is to get away from the old folks—a situation not wholly without parallel among higher organisms.

Among animals this competitive destruction of the young by the old is not so obvious. On the contrary, as we ascend the scale of animal evolution we find relentless destruction being supplanted by positive care, protection, and nourishment. The effectiveness of this protection, and the duration of the period of true infancy, is one of the best single tests of evolutionary advancement. It is upon this basis that mammals may claim to be the highest type of life. This upward progression is marked by a decreased birth rate, which in one aspect appears as a necessary condition for full parental care, and in another aspect may be regarded a measure of economy whereby the survival of the species is guaranteed by carefully cherishing a few offspring, rather than by producing multitudinous offspring and leaving the outcome to chance.

But, long or short, the period of infancy eventually comes to an end, and parental sacrifice is supplanted by parental rivalry. It has been said—by Ernest Seton Thompson, was it not?—that no wild animal dies a natural death. This means that in the fierce struggle for existence any minor indisposition, injury, or weakness, not sufficient in itself to cause death, is enough to turn the balance against the affected individual and crowd him to the wall. It is just another way of stating the law of the survival of the fittest. And chief among the agents that eliminate the unfit are always the young, vigorous, aggressive members of the same species.

Among animals, furthermore, we find some instances of positive, direct killing of the young by their parents, or at least by the older generation. One remarkable example is furnished by the giant salamander, Cryptobranchus. The male of this species sets himself on guard over the eggs, protecting them from attack. But his attitude is not wholly disinterested, for at the same time he is protecting his food supply. Both he and the female devour the eggs greedily, and only their slow rate of digestion permits the larger portion of the eggs to be safely hatched. Certain kinds of fish feed upon the young of the same species. Even among human beings, it is sometimes customary for the victim of infanticide to be eaten by its mother for the purpose of recovering the strength she has given it.

It appears, then, that this phenomenon of the killing of the young by the old and the old by the young is a virtually universal characteristic of organisms in nature. It must, therefore, rest upon a broad instinctive basis, in fact upon some impulses that reach down to the very lowest levels of organic existence. There are just two impulses that are common to all living things; the impulse to take nourishment and the impulse to procreate—hunger and love. The truth is that the phenomenon in question is the logical outcome of a perennial clash between these two impulses.

III

Practically every list of instincts starts with hunger and love, and practically all students of behavior regard these two impulses as the primary springs of action. Yet there has been apparently very little recognition of the fact that between hunger and love there exists an inherent and inveterate antagonism. Hunger exists as a necessary requirement for the survival of the individual; love is indispensable for the continuance of the species. Nature (if she may be personified) is vastly more interested in the perpetuation of the species than in the survival of the individual. The one great thing towards which she labors is that out of each generation enough should grow up to maturity to take the places left vacant by the death of the elders. She is seemingly quite indifferent to the wastefulness of the methods by which this result is secured. If it is necessary that two of the offspring of each female oyster shall survive to take the places of their parents, Nature regards with complete complacence the birth of sixteen million oysters out of whom 15,999,-998 are doomed to die, most of them in early infancy. The life cycle of many organisms seems to have procreation as its one outstanding and final objective.

But while Nature is thus superlatively solicitous about the survival of each species, she cares nothing at all about the increase of any species once it has been established. Producing new life with a lavishness beyond human imagination, she makes no provision whatever for permanent increase in the total of life. The cosmic supplies by which Nature supports her creatures are absolutely fixed and limited in both quantity and quality. Having served their purpose in maintaining life they are returned to the great storehouse to meet future requisitions. Thus life may go on perennially, but the total volume of life, once reached, can never be increased. And it is safe to say that the total volume under natural conditions was reached long before the appearance of man.

The rule of Nature, therefore, is that parents are continually bringing into the world multitudinous offspring, most of whom they will destroy, and the survivors of whom will eventually destroy them. From the point of view of material well-being parents and children are implacable enemies. As far as individual comfort is concerned, creatures in nature would be better off if they bore no children at all. Yet in spite of this fact, and doubtless, from the evolutionary standpoint, because of this fact, they are equipped with an irresistible impulse that drives them to bear children continuously up to the very limit of their physiological capacity. Is it any wonder that this is a world of struggle, when the two basic impulses of life are set against each other in such an eternal conflict? It is well that those who insistently demand the rule of nature in human affairs should reflect upon this situation. If man is ever fully to vindicate his humanity he must find a counteragent for this relationship. For the basic factors in the situation are not altered in the least when we enter the human arena. The impulses to seek food and to seek mates are not one whit diminished. In fact, the latter is apparently largely extended. The ultimate supplies of nature, out of which human life must be maintained, are not one atom enlarged. Men are still impelled to bring into the world many more offspring than can be supported, and there is still the incentive for parents to destroy children, children to destroy parents.

The novel factors which differentiate the human aspects of this problem from the purely natural are of two main types. In the first place, man, by developing an economic culture, has continuously and progressively increased the supporting power of the land from his own point of view, and so has been able to provide for a gradual and eventually notable increase in numbers. This process has consisted largely in the substitution of human life for other forms of life. Perhaps there has also been an increase in the total volume of life (a difficult thing to reduce to concrete measurement) through the better utilization of the natural elements. In the second place, there has been developed a love for children, and pleasure in children, which serves as a motive alongside of the pleasure in material things. It is still true of human individuals, as of other organisms, that from the purely materialistic point of view they would be better off if they bore no children at all. But "man does not live by bread alone," and to the normal man the joys and satisfactions of children rank high among the things that make life worth living. On the one hand, accordingly, man has been able to provide for a continuous increase in numbers living on a steadily advancing level of comfort, and on the other hand he has enjoyed from his children satisfactions that to some degree at least compensate for the loss in physical comfort that children involve.

In spite of all this, however, if it were possible to survey the whole career of mankind, it would probably be found that the social situations in which these two factors taken together were sufficient to neutralize the inherent antagonism between hunger and love have been very restricted in area and limited in time. In other words, there have been relatively very few societies in which the typical parents, from their own personal point of view, have wanted as many children as they were physiologically capable of producing, or as many as the unrestrained yielding to the procreative impulse would naturally bring into being. Conversely, there have been very few societies in which the support of the old folks was not felt as a burden; a burden in some cases made welcome by filial affection, in some cases endured with more or less good grace because of the pressure of social convention or moral standards. That this contention holds for practically all savage and barbaric societies is evidenced by the universality of the customs already described. It is not so easy to see that it is true among the most advanced representatives of modern civilization.

IV

It is particularly difficult for members of the society called the United States to accept the existence of this fundamental conflict. This is partly because the frank discussion of such matters is put under powerful taboos. This applies not only to matters of sex, but to all matters that conduce to a pessimistic view of human, and particularly national, affairs. As Professor Sumner says, "Our civilization ordinarily veils from us the fact that we are rivals and enemies to each other in the competition of life." More important than this is the fact that we, as a nation, have lived for so many generations upon a surplus economy, and upon an economic system in which children very early become a financial asset, that an increasing population has been tacitly assumed to be a benefit, and the drain of large families has not been heavily felt. America represents the acme of conditions under which this antagonism is reduced to its minimum proportions. Yet even here there is abundant evidence that the rivalry between children and parents exists, and is quite generally felt. According to some students, even in the nineteenth century a large proportion of the births represented unwanted children. "An eminent physician once said that in his experience every one ardently desired the first child, nearly every one the second, the majority the third, few the fourth and fifth, and no one the sixth. This may be stretching things a little at both ends, but there is no doubt of its approximate correctness." It is true that there is no socially sanctioned and ceremonial killing of either the young or the old. Our whole culture is based on the sanctity and inviolability of every human life, whether it represents an economic asset or a liability. But there is evidence that the killing of the young in the pre-natal period is a widespread practice, winked at if not sanctioned by society. Obviously exact statistics on the question are an impossibility, but the estimates accepted by supposedly careful students range from half a million to two million annually in the United States. By others, these figures, except perhaps the lowest, are regarded as wild exaggerations, but there can be no doubt that the actual total would be impressive. In any case, we should not fall into national self-complacency on this matter, recognizing that it is our economic good fortune more than anything else that differentiates us in this particular from China, where infanticide is so well known, or India, of which W. J. Wilkins is quoted as saying that "six sevenths of the population of India have for ages practiced female infanticide." Nor should we fall into the illusion that some special Providence, without any cooperation on our part, will preserve us from the conditions which drive irresistibly toward some expedients to mitigate the basic conflict. In point of fact, the average individual family has no difficulty in recognizing this antithesis. Its adult members are used to thinking in terms of a definite income, difficult to increase, and certainly not directly affected in a favorable manner by the advent of a new member of the family. With a fixed income, the material well-being of each member of the family becomes a matter of simple division. Without giving much reflection to the matter, even the least intelligent parents recognize that additional children mean additional burdens and lower the general level of comfort of the family. They accept the situation partly through sheer fatalism, partly because they do not know what they can do about it, partly because they find compensation in the joys that come from children, and very largely because they regard children as a form of insurance against destitution in their own declining years—support of the old having been substituted for slaughter of the old in our modern mores.

It is when we turn to the broader social aspects of the matter that we find the problem clouded in mists of ignorance, misinterpretation, and baseless tradition. Western societies for centuries past have been governed by the doctrine, widely disseminated and unquestioningly accepted, that a large and increasing population is a desirable thing from the group point of view. The origin of this tradition may be traced to a complex of factors: dynastic ambition, religious aggrandizement, family pride, false economic theories, and sound militaristic principles. The common man, sufficiently acute to realize the antagonism between a growing family and his own creature comfort, has been educated by those who control public opinion and sentiment to believe that the interests of his group are differently served from his own, and to consider that each additional member of his family, however well or ill supported, is a positive contribution to the welfare of his society. There is thus added another offsetting reward—the sense of social approval and self-approbation for a duty well done—to help compensate him for a diminution in his own material well-being. So thoroughly has this work of education been done that to the man on the street the desirability of an increasing population seems almost axiomatic. His first—often his only—interest in the newly published census report is to see whether his own city, his own state, his own nation has grown, and how much. His reaction to evidence of rapid growth in any one of these aggregates is quite different from his feeling about the same development in his own family.

Most of us have not been impressed by the fact that the relation of increasing population to material comfort is a problem in division in a society just as truly as in a family. There is, indeed, this difference that the new member of the family is likely to leave the family very soon after he becomes able to add to its income, and so is not thought of as a means of increasing the amount to be divided, whereas he remains a member of the society during an extended productive period. Thus a growing population means not only more persons among whom to distribute the social product but a larger social product to be distributed. If the man on the street were able to analyze his feeling about population he would probably find that if it has any tangible basis at all it is in a tacit assumption that each increment produces as much as it consumes or possibly more. If this were true, there would be no conflict between hunger and love on the societal plane. Unfortunately this is not universally true, and has been true in fact in only extremely rare cases and for very brief periods of time. The situation has become standardized in that commonplace of economic theory, the Law of Diminishing Returns. Economic production is the result of the combination of various factors, primary among which is land. Because the elemental constituents of the land are fixed and immutable it results that while additional applications of labor and capital will produce a larger gross product they cannot be made indefinitely to produce a larger proportional product, or even the same proportional product. Eventually the time comes when each increment of labor and capital produces a progressively diminishing proportional product. Stated as a matter of population increase, this means that the time comes in every society when each future increment in population means a smaller *per capita* share of the total social product.

V

The clash between hunger and love accordingly expresses itself on the societal plane in terms of population and standard of living. If a society could improve, or even maintain, its standard of living in the face of uncontrolled growth of population there would be no social discord between the basic impulses of life. The outstanding lesson of history is that this can be done only under most exceptional circumstances, and then for only a very limited space of time. This situation is characteristic of a genuinely underpopulated society. Such a group has not people enough to achieve its maximum standard of living. Such a situation is self-corrective. The personal as well as the social advantages that accrue from increasing numbers serve to remove some of the customary barriers to population growth—including any traces of sanctioned killing that may survive—and the forces of reproduction, freed from restraint, fill up the deficiency with amazing rapidity. Probably the United States furnishes the most remarkable illustration of these processes that the world has ever known or will ever know. Canada, Australia, and some of the South American countries furnish other examples on a smaller scale or less fully developed.

The vitally important truth is that the situation in all of these countries is necessarily temporary. The extraordinary economic history of the United States represents a suspension, not an abrogation, of the fundamental law of conflict between hunger and love. We have no more reason to hope that without taking thought—that is, without intelligent, scientific social engineering—we can enjoy a suspension of this law forever than that China and India will mysteriously be granted exemption from it within the next generation.

Left to themselves, the forces of hunger and of love, in the human arena no less than in nature, lead inevitably to struggle, and struggle leads inevitably to killing. The career of man on earth is scarcely less an orgy of killing than that of the lower organisms in nature. Among men, too, this slaughter takes two forms; the passive, persistent form—economic competition, and the violent aggressive form—war. Which of the two, among men, has more victims to its credit it would be difficult to say. Putting them all together—infanticide, abortion, starvation, war—it is distressingly evident that man has only very partially emancipated himself from the fundamental conditions of organic life.

Yet man alone, of all living creatures, holds the key to the dilemma. He alone has the power to adjust the growth of his species to the material supplies that can be made available without invoking the grim expedient of slaughter. Only man has the capacity to foresee the consequences of mating, to differentiate between the desire for children (apparently an exclusively human endowment) and the desire for mating, and so to regulate his behavior that the only children that are born shall be wanted children; that is, children who are the result of the desire for children, not of blind obedience to impulse.

The first step in bringing about this happy consummation is the effective establishment of the idea that uncontrolled hunger and uncontrolled love are mutually antagonistic on the social as well as the personal plane. Intelligent nations must be brought to realize that unless they are definitely underpopulated increases in population not only menace their own economic prosperity, but inescapably threaten their peaceful relations with other nations. Whether the United States has already passed beyond the stage of underpopulation is a debatable question. There is strong evidence that she has. At any rate the time is not far distant when she will, and it is none too early to begin to devise means to get the situation in hand. On the basis of a popularized recognition of the undesirability of increase in population, nations can develop new social standards, new canons of morality, new conventions, new criteria of national prosperity, which will very speedily produce their reactions upon individual ideas and individual behavior. It is not beyond belief that in time this new social outlook may produce a type of culture, at least among the more advanced nations, wherein the reproduction of the species will naturally and subconsciously, without undue hardship or felt repression, be adjusted to the existing economic conditions in such a way as to promote the maximum standard of living—and the conflict between hunger and love will be outlawed.

10

LABOR V. LEISURE

Written in 1931

THE GOSPEL of Work! How familiarly its slogans ring in our ears: "If any would not work, neither should he eat." "For Satan finds some mischief still for idle hands to do." "In work that keeps faith sweet and strong." "The right to work."

From time immemorial work has been glorified. Song and story yield their homage to the solid merits of work, however romantically they may extol the delights of indolence, while essay and biography axiomatically acclaim work as the sure means to personal success and social esteem. The more prosaic and academic discussions of contemporary life, in their exaltation of work as the great social panacea, do but re-echo the words of Carlyle, who describes it as "The grand cure of all the maladies and miseries that ever beset mankind." The Rotarian mind makes work co-equal, if not identical, with service. Nowhere has this doctrine been better summed up than in the words of that past master of pious platitudes, Calvin Coolidge: "To provide for the economic well-being of our inhabitants, only three attributes, which are not beyond the reach of the average person, are necessary—honesty, industry, and thrift." (Oh, if it were only so simple.)

Yet in this year of unemployment, nineteen hundred and thirty-one, the one word that is on every expositor's tongue is "Overproduction." It is overproduction that is the cause of the business depression, of unemployment, of the collapse of the stock market, of international friction—industrial overproduction, agricultural overproduction, overproduction of everything in general. Shades of the Classical Economists! What has become of the elaborate argument that they were so learnedly developing scarcely a century ago proving that general overproduction is an impossibility, and which is still the stock in trade of most of the teachers of conventional economics to-day?

Now when you look at it squarely, what is overproduction but the tangible consequence of too much work? Here is surely a rare paradox. Work the great panacea, overproduction the besetting malady. Yet the characteristic features of the disease are the logical result of the remedy. There must be something wrong with this picture.

The simple fact is, that the current social concept of work and the usual personal attitude toward it are two items in our traditional impedimenta which must be completely revolutionized to fit the conditions of modern times. "Honesty, industry, and thrift" have had a long and honorable career and have rendered yeoman service in the evolution of human welfare. Doubtless, honesty is still a serviceable virtue, where it can be found. But industry and thrift have outlived their pristine usefulness, and ought to be put on part time.

For about 999,950 years the chief preoccupation of man has been getting a living. The bare task of keeping soul and body together, and providing himself with a few simple comforts and an occasional modest luxury or two, has engrossed his entire time and energy. The one imperious demand that Nature made of him was work. There was a direct and conspicuous relationship between the amount of work he did and his chance of survival, not to speak of any positive enjoyment or contentment. Society needed the full output of the productive energy of every one of its adult members, however unevenly the product of that energy may have been distributed. Starvation was never far from the lower classes, want from the middle groups, or privation from the privileged. Famine was something more than a remote possibility. During this long period the utility of work was so great that reverence for it became so thoroughly ingrained in human nature as to seem almost instinctive, and social sanctions in favor of work were developed of the most imperious character.

Now, within the last fifty years, man suddenly finds himself possessed of a productive mechanism so capacious and competent that if he expends his habitual amount of work on it will swamp him with more goods than he has the ability to grapple with. No wonder many of his traditional values seem all awry! No wonder he stands trembling, bemused, awestruck before his own devices, the wise use of which defies his intelligence, the power of which far outstrips his ability to control.

In June, 1918, Mr. H. L. Gantt, one of the foremost efficiency engineers this country has ever known, said, "On the whole, only about fifty per cent of our industrial machines are actually operating during the time they are expected to operate, and on the whole these machines, during the time they are being operated, are producing only about fifty per cent of what they are expected to produce. This brings our productive result down to about one-fourth of what it might be if the machines were run all of the time at their highest capacity."

This was during war time. Millions of men were engaged in military (largely wealth-destroying) activities, and other millions of workers were occupied in extraordinary lines of production necessitated by the military situation. Yet in spite of these handicaps, the operation of our machines at one-fourth capacity resulted in such accumulations of goods that they were an embarrassment to government officials for years after peace was restored. It is quite a conservative estimate that if all our productive plant were operated at its maximum efficiency we could turn out more goods than we now know how to dispose of wisely with an average working day for all the available labor of not more than four hours.

In brief, we have achieved a New Freedom beside which the paltry emancipation usually referred to by that term is trivial and insignificant—the Freedom from the incessant task of making a living, the Freedom to *live*. But we have not yet learned what to do with it. We keep on working because we don't know how to stop.

II

One factor that hampers our readjustment to the new situation, and which is itself a consequence of our age-long subjection to work, is an extraordinary inversion in our conception of production and consumption. The origin of this is natural enough. As primitive man, gradually emerging from the shadows of savagery, began to catch a vision of the capacity of material things to gratify human wants, he became acutely conscious of the fact that one great limitation to his enjoyment was his meager ability to produce these devices. He learned by experience that the surest way to enlarge his equipment for happiness was to improve his productive technic. Thus he came to regard increased production as an end in itself because the results of production were so easily taken for granted. He did not perceive that there was a necessary and natural limit to the principle. Consequently, when the Industrial Revolution came along, with its unprecedented expansion of productive capacity, instead of causing mankind to turn its attention to the ultimate ends and purposes of production, it raised the adulation of production to the nth degree. Western society became completely hypnotized by its new powers and followed blindly in whatever direction the new machines and factories and consolidations and expansions happened to lead.

This perverted attitude was caught up, systematized, and standardized by the contemporary leaders of social thought, so that the whole characteristic economic doctrine and teaching of the nineteenth century were completely dominated by the beneficence of productive devices and activities. This philosophy has been admirably and ironically summed up by James MacKaye in his little book, "The Happiness of Nations" (a title obviously chosen as an antithesis to Adam Smith's famous work): "Wealth is a means to happiness. The more wealth there is, the greater will be the happiness. Consequently, to be as happy as possible, spend as much time as possible producing wealth."

So, by the beginning of the twentieth century, the people of the Western world were thoroughly trained to think of themselves as producers, but were completely untutored with respect to their capacities as consumers—in fact, almost never received the slightest encouragement to think of themselves in that light. The whole philosophy of the contemporary Western world is a producers' philosophy.

Expressions and applications of this outlook abound on every hand. On almost every important economic question practically all the arguments, on both sides, are based upon the importance of production and consideration of the producer, and either completely ignore, or at best simply take for granted, consumption and consumer. The most conspicuous example of this generalization is, of course, the tariff. The whole defense of this incredible monstrosity is built upon the necessity of cherishing and fostering the productive interests of the country—individual producers, producing classes, the nation as a producer. But every single argument in favor of protection has an equally weighty, and much more logical, rebuttal when viewed from the standpoint of the consumer but we seldom hear the latter. One of the redeeming features of conventional economics is that, for the most part, it does teach free trade; but the prevailing business dogmas are too strong for the academic economists.

Another vastly significant case in point is the typical business man's attitude toward wages. Wages appear to him as an important item in the cost of production. Only recently has he begun to glimpse the fact that wages are an identically important factor in the consuming power of the market. The first thing the average employer does in a period of overproduction like the present is to pare down the pay-roll as near to the core as possible, forgetting that in so doing he is intensifying the evils of under-consumption, which are the real root of the trouble. All practices aiming at the limitation of output, whether engaged in by employers or laborers, are based on the same conception. The great question is, "How can I best serve myself and other producers?"

This attitude was variously and vigorously expounded during the years of the great fight for the restriction of immigration. All the economic arguments of the "liberal" camp were based on recognition of the immigrant as a producer—it occurred to none of them to remember that he was exactly as much a consumer.

Recent striking examples of the situation have been furnished by the alleged "dumping" of wheat in America, and cheap electric-light bulbs in England, by the Soviet Republic. This has been axiomatically regarded as a dastardly deed. The Bolshevists have been held up to withering scorn and contumely for making it possible for American consumers to buy wheat and Englishmen to buy lamps cheaper than would otherwise have been the case.

To be sure, within the last few years there have been a few gleams of light on the horizon. A number of books have been written that recognize consumption as an important social phenomenon, and particularly the work of Stuart Chase is doing much to educate the public to think of themselves as consumers. We not infrequently hear the present economic situation referred to as a period of "under-consumption" rather than "over-production." Manufacturers and advertising men have begun to recognize that the consumer exists, and must be taken into consideration. The doctrine that prosperity depends upon increased consumption of goods has been diligently preached by Foster and Catchings and others, and has enjoyed a good deal of popularity. But even so, the consumer has been almost invariably brought into the picture as a stimulus, a prerequisite, a sine qua non, to production. Thus Garet Garrett: "To be able to say in the evening, 'I have consumed more to-day than I consumed yesterday'—this now is a duty the individual owes to industrial society." Fancy the *duty* of consumption!

All our high-pressure salesmanship is devoted to stimulating consumption, not in the least in order that the consumer may be happier, or healthier, or more contented, but that he may multiply the possibilities of production. Says Ralph Borsodi, "No matter how much the consumer who can afford to pay may resist, he must be made to eat more, to wear out more clothes, to take more drugs, to blow out more tires. He must consume, consume, consume, so that our industries may produce, produce, produce."

It will take Herculean efforts to reverse this attitude, and accustom ourselves to thinking of ourselves as consumers, and of production as the humble handmaiden of consumption, justified and tolerable only to the extent that it genuinely subserves the consumptive requirements of the human personality. But this must be done before we can even begin to reap the full advantage of our New Freedom.

Hand in hand with admiration for work, naturally, has gone condemnation of idleness. In Western countries idleness has been habitually regarded as a vice, just like drunkenness or gambling. Numerous laws have penalized the idle on the same terms as serious criminals. Every proposal for the shortening of the working day of the common laborer has always been vigorously opposed as yielding too much leisure, to be expended in the demoralizing and depraving pursuits of idleness. "Spare time" has been considered as something dangerous, or at best irksome. It has been something to be disposed of, to be got rid of with the least possible effort and disturbance.

Among the staunchest devotees of the god of work has been the Christian religion. As so frequently happens, religion has espoused a doctrine that already enjoyed full social sanction, and has given it back to the community with the added weight of divine support and approval. Work has been presented as a pious duty. This was conspicuously illustrated in the case of the Protestant founders of this country. Starting with the assumption that the Lord would provide for his own in material ways as well as spiritual ("Yet, have I not seen the righteous forsaken nor his seed begging bread," "The righteous shall inherit the earth"), it was an easy step to the conclusion that the degree of worldly prosperity enjoyed by an individual was a measure of his favor with the Lord. And from this it was a simple deduction that the pursuit of wealth was one form of service to God. And this meant work.

We all remember with what gusto we used to sing the good old Gospel Hymn that adjured us to "Work, for the night is coming, Work mid springing flowers . . . . Work through the sunny noon" (no time off for lunch), and so on till we finished "under the sunset skies," having fulfilled perfectly the injunction to "fill brightest hours with labor." And all for what? What was the reward? "Rest comes sure and soon." Work in order that you may rest, rest in order that you may work! What are sparkling dew, springing flowers, radiant sunsets, all the splendors of glorious Nature for but to work in?

And so illustrations might be multiplied indefinitely—the New York Times editorially heralding the discovery that work is no longer a curse but a blessing—just because, forsooth, without work many persons cannot fill their stomachs; a popular magazine paying money to advertise the doctrine that "Economic America has no other problem than that of getting enough of its commodities into the hands of the masses of wage-earning America in order to keep the wheels of its mass production turning at the other end." But enough! The existing situation should be sufficiently clear. The great question is, what are we going to do about it?

III

What is needed is obviously a revolution in some of our basic philosophies of life. First of all, as already intimated, we must have a complete reversal of our characteristic attitude toward economic activities. The god of work must be cast down from his ancient throne, and the divinity of enjoyment put in his place. We must learn that consumption is the only justification and guide of production. We must learn that consumption requires the same scientific study and research that we have so generously lavished on production. We must develop a technic of consumption. Hitherto we have relied upon the assumption that human beings know by intuition or instinct how to utilize the products of their own inventive achievements. This is utterly false. Our instincts trace back to our cave ancestors or their simian forbears. It is just as absurd to suppose that a man knows intuitively how most efficiently to enjoy a radio or an automobile as that he knows instinctively how to operate a steam shovel or a linotype. We must develop first a sound theory of consumption, and then a system of education and training for consumption.

Along with this, we must have a new philosophy of work. Work must be recognized not as a virtue or a blessing, but as an intrinsic evil. The only justification for work is its product. Work is a means to an end, and the end should govern the means. To be sure, it should be remembered that there may be, and often are, useful products of work aside from the ostensible and direct object of the work—by-products, as it were. There is doubtless a high disciplinary value, and often an intense personal satisfaction, in tackling a hard job, throwing all one's energies and capacities into it, and seeing it through to a successful conclusion, or even, in case of failure, realizing that one has done the best he could. But to secure these benefits, work must be voluntary, intelligent, purposeful, and essentially self-directed. These characteristics are conspicuously absent from a large portion of modern industrial work. Very frequently the machine worker of to-day does not even know what he is making or what its relation is to any general scheme of things.

Sometimes, too, there is pleasure in the very work itself. To the extent that this is true, the activity ceases to be work in the strict sense of the word. Or perhaps it would be more accurate to say that the satisfaction which justifies the work comes directly, without the mediation of any concrete product of work. One man works hard in an office all the week so that he may play golf on Saturday afternoons and Sundays; another man becomes a golf professional from the sheer love of the game. These are simply two different ways of getting satisfaction from work.

In the new day work must not only not be encouraged but not permitted unless there is some positive and demonstrable social good to be derived from it. Work is too potent a thing to be indulged in irresponsibly. We can't allow people to go about working at their own sweet will.

We must have a new philosophy of thrift. In the old days saving was practiced to provide against want or dependency in old age or to substitute future enjoyment for present. A small part of saving is still for these purposes, and that part is fully justified. But most modern saving is for investment, and investment means more machines and more productive plant, and so more potentialities of work. People in the future will not be allowed to save and invest recklessly.

We must have a new philosophy of waste. In the past waste has been considered as almost a mortal sin, virtually equivalent to a form of robbery. The assumption has been that the waster keeps somebody else from getting goods that he otherwise would have enjoyed, or possibly that waste makes somebody work harder than he otherwise would need to. But under modern conditions waste is not necessarily an evil; it may be a distinct benefit. There are two types of waste which should be clearly distinguished. The first is waste which tends to deplete the natural resources of the land more rapidly than necessary. This is emphatically an evil—if anything, a more flagrant evil to-day than ever before. It *is* a form of robbery—the robbery of unborn generations. The other form of waste is simply the consumption of a certain commodity with less ultimate satisfaction than it is capable of yielding. If this means merely the arbitrary destruction of a part of the surplus product of past work it may be positively beneficial, by making a larger place for the product of the work that is now going on.

We must, most emphatically of all, have a new philosophy of idleness—or rather, we must substitute for the present philosophy of idleness a sound and comprehensive philosophy of leisure time. We must come to realize that lesure time, that is, time spent in pleasureable employment, is the only kind of time that makes life worth living. All other time is tolerable only as it contributes to the richness and developmental content of our leisure. But, of course, leisure, to be itself tolerable, must be immeasurably more than mere idleness. Leisure time should mean the opportunity for all those pursuits that really contribute to the realization and enlargement of personality. Many of these activities, in the case of certain individuals, may, as has already been intimated, bear the outward semblance of work. Every amateur photographer, cabinet maker, or gardener knows this. The distinction between work time and leisure time depends not on what is done but why it is done.

In this connection, the phrase "idle rich" must lose its current uncomplimentary significance. Idle is exactly what the rich ought to be. Idle, of course, in the sense that they are not doing remunerative work of a kind that keeps somebody else from getting the income that he can get only from work. Let us desist from lauding the scion of a wealthy family who puts on overalls and goes out to take his part in the "work of the world." There is not work enough to go around, and he already has his share of the good things of life. Let him devote his time to some noncompetitive pursuit—art, or philosophy, or research, or the breeding of Chow dogs or dahlias, or what you will—and leave work to those who have to have it.

One final requirement—we must have a new philosophy of education. There has been endless argumentation about the purpose and the end of education. One of the most modern and popular theories is that education is to teach us to think. To-day this doctrine is wholly inadequate. The purpose of education should be to train us to *live*. Thinking is a part of the art of living, but it is by no means all of it. We already have machines to do a good deal of our thinking for us. What we need to learn is what life is really for, what it has potentially to offer, what is its relative scale of values. What changes this new concept may induce in the average curriculum time alone can tell. But the change in basis for evaluating courses is revolutionary. Education in the past has been almost exclusively focussed on work time; the education of the future must be centered on leisure time. As already intimated, a part of this new system of education must be the development of an inclusive theoretical science and practical art of consumption. This will involve the working out of formulas to enable us to establish the correct ratios between productive time and consumptive time. We must learn to recognize that consumption takes time just as truly as production, and we must discover precisely the amount of productive time which is required, under varying social and economic conditions, to provide just that combination of material goods and leisure time that will yield the maximum degree of satisfaction in consumption.

And when this is all done, when all these philosophical revolutions have been accomplished, and their teachings put into effect, we shall probably discover that work, in the ancient sense of the word, has almost disappeared, vanished into thin air. All the drudgery, all the dirty and disagreeable tasks, will be done by machinery, and the others will have lost the characteristic features of work. The machines will be so intelligently administered that they will operate only in such ways and for such periods of time as are necessary to turn out the goods required for the most efficient consumption of the community. The residuum of activity still necessary to be done by human agencies will be so limited in quantity, and so evenly distributed among all the individuals in the community, that it will be at worst neutral, and for the most part positively pleasurable. For, as already observed, the distinction between work and play is not what is done but how, to what extent, and for what purpose it is done. There is practically nothing which is done by masses of people as work that is not also done by individuals for pleasure and recreation. When mechanization has been carried to its ultimate perfection there will be so little of routine production left for human hands and minds to do that in all probability there will be actual competition for the doing of it for its own sake, for the interest, variety, and stimulation that it has to offer.

Thus the distinction between work and recreation will at last be wiped out altogether. Everyone will be left free for genuinely creative activities. Type will still be set, clothes made, furniture built, gardens planted, and ditches dug by hand. But these things will be done in just the same spirit as now pictures are painted, songs sung, and doilies embroidered—for the delight and pleasure in doing them, for the expression and development of personality. Few enjoyments are higher than those which come from impressing one's own individuality upon a material medium, especially if it be in measurably permanent form. Mankind is endowed with limitless capacities for creating beautiful and useful things in varied and individual forms. The men of the future—and not such a distant future, either—will devote themselves to these and kindred pursuits, and will look back upon their ancestors who spent their time and energy in the routine production of standardized, conventional, and largely superfluous material objects in much the same attitude with which we regard the savages who knock out their teeth, brand their skin, or cut off the joints of their fingers for some traditional reason that they do not even think of trying to understand, but just blindly obey.

11

WILL THE WAGE SYSTEM LAST?

Written in 1920

We are often told that men's political and economic theories are nothing more than attempts to state or explain social conditions as they exist at the time being; that theories change with changing conditions, and that a change in facts always precedes a change in theory. This is doubtless true to a large extent. Just as in the realm of physical science the hypothesis or theory which, when sufficiently verified, becomes a "natural law" is only our formulation of what has been observed uniformly to happen, so in the field of social relations any general theory or law is a statement of what transpires with regularity under a given set of conditions.

From this premise there is frequently drawn the corollary that since today's theories are the result of today's facts they can therefore have no causative relation to the facts of tomorrow, and that accordingly political and economic theories have only academic interest, serving to explain to the inquiring mind the course of events which move on by their own momentum, but having no bearing upon what that course shall be. This doctrine is profoundly false. It ignores the fundamental distinction between the physical and social sciences, which is that the unit particles in the field of social phenomena are, in some sense, self-governing, which we do not grant to atoms or molecules. All strictly social phenomena, therefore—all the things which differentiate a human society from an unintelligent organism, a coral reef, or a pack of wolves—arise from the *willed* acts of human beings. Every volitional act, in turn, of an individual arises from a belief, and the volitional acts of groups of individuals are the direct results of a consensus of beliefs which we call a social theory.

So true is this that Norman Angell, the keenness of whose political insight the war has amply demonstrated, takes as the text of one of his most significant chapters the statement by another author that "Not the facts, but men's opinions about the facts, are what matter." Men act in the light of what they think about the facts. That their thoughts may be entirely unsound and unwarranted by the facts makes no difference. To be sure, to the extent that men are intelligent, and can learn by experience, their beliefs and theories are eventually checked up against the facts, and corrected. But the process takes a long time and is always far from complete. At any given time the course of social evolution is controlled and directed very largely by beliefs which, though widely held, are erroneous.

History, ancient and modern, furnishes a multiplicity of verifications of this truth. Two examples will suffice. For countless centuries it was believed in the most civilized countries that severe punishments, particularly if publicly administered, would act as a deterrent to crime. Henry VIII of England was a firm devotee of this theory, with the result that 72,000 persons were hanged in the course of his reign. A remarkable passage from a letter of instructions to one of his Dukes makes it clear that his severity was supported by his belief that disloyalty would be reduced thereby. This belief has been one of the hardest for men to abandon. If crime failed to decrease under a certain set of laws it was assumed that the punishment was not severe enough, and the penalties were increased. Within a few months from this writing, a convict was hanged in a Chicago prison in the sight of the rest of the prisoners, in the belief that it would tend to make them "lead better lives." The most advanced theory of today is that severe punishments, especially if publicly executed, tend to *increase* crime. Assuming that this new theory represents the facts, its acceptance today will lead to a sounder and more humane procedure in the future, though it cannot restore the lives of the hundreds of thousands of victims of the old mistaken theory.

For a hundred years and more myriads of immigrants from Europe have braved hardship, privation, and uncertainty to cross the Atlantic and take up residence on the North American continent. This great social phenomenon—the most spectacular population movement of all time—has rested entirely on human belief, the belief that in the new world the immigrant would find increased happiness, prosperity, or contentment. In countless cases this belief was substantiated by subsequent facts. In thousands of other cases the belief was erroneous, resting upon the glowing delineations of the steamship agents rather than upon truth. But in every case it was the belief, not the accuracy or falsity of the belief, that determined conduct, and gave its character to this stupendous movement. In the meantime, the people of the United States as a whole, though warned by an occasional protesting voice, have acted upon the theory that there was a magical potency in American life which was taking these aliens and smoothly and efficiently transforming them and absorbing them into the body politic, after the figure of the melting pot. This theory dominated our policy for many decades, and it took the great cataclysm of the war to reveal even to "the wayfaring man, though a fool" how thoroughly out of conformity to the facts it was. Now we have swung around, and are trying to avert the consequences of a mistaken theory by the harsh and drastic expedient of wholesale deportations. We *believe* that this will help to remedy the situation. Time may prove that we are wrong. But until it does, we can only act upon what seems the best theory.

Herein lies the great danger of democracy. In the days of Henry VIII the beliefs of one man were the important thing. In every oligarchy the theories of a few determine events. But the safety of a democracy demands the most unflagging zeal for the universal dissemination of correct political theories, and the universal recognition of the necessity of constantly checking up the theories, however fondly cherished and widely accepted, against the ever changing conditions of a dynamic society. This is something that men hate to do. Having once worked out a theory which satisfactorily explains the facts of a given epoch, they are reluctant to abandon it, and when it becomes evident that facts are changing so as to undermine the theory, there is a tendency to resent the change and to attempt to prevent the alterations in fact for the sake of preserving the theory. This is a highly dangerous procedure. For a social theory tenaciously held after the conditions which justified it have disappeared may retard progress indefinitely and may transform a smooth, orderly process of evolution into a bitter and catastrophic upheaval.

II

Of all the social sciences, probably economics is considered, and rightly, to have approached most closely the exactitude and fixity of the physical sciences. We are accustomed to think of the law of supply and demand as immutable and absolute, like the laws of gravitation or chemical affinity. Thus a writer in a recent number of the Unpartisan Review: "Sentiment is as helpless in the presence of economic forces as it is in the presence of the law of gravitation." Of course every student of economics recognizes that many of the economic theories of the past were mistaken and have had to be corrected; he may even admit that the best theories of the present may need to be modified and amended in the light of farther facts. But most of us are inclined to assume that back of our human formulation of economic laws there are eternal verities in which we can place the same confidence that we do in the basic forces of the physical universe. It is a wholesome thing to realize that this assumption, if true at all, is true only to a limited extent. The laws of economics must be regarded as tentative and transitory, not only because it is exceedingly difficult to study economic facts by strictly scientific methods, but because the facts themselves—the volitional wealth-seeking activities of human beings—are subject to unpredictable changes. Of course the only economic theories that have any influence worth considering are of the type already described—a consensus of belief or group opinion—not the kind that some individual works out by the armchair method.

For instance, one of the stock arguments against socialism as an economic system has always been that with the removal of the motive of financial self-interest production would suffer from the lack of an adequate incentive. But the war showed us that under favorable conditions the desire for public service, at least when coupled with the need of self-defense, will drive men to more arduous and efficient efforts than the lure of wealth. Until we can be positive that the motive of public service can never become generally operative under peace conditions, this argument against socialism is not conclusive, though perhaps such an outcome, even as a possibility, is too far in the future to justify practical interest. Again, it is a startling but incontestable fact that if the simplest principles of Christianity—"whatsoever ye would that men should do to you, do ye even so to them," "thou shalt love thy neighbor as thyself," "it is more blessed to give than to receive"—should ever be generally accepted (a thing which, however improbable, we are not yet ready to admit unthinkable) every economics textbook in use would have to be thrown into the waste-basket. Our whole economic theory is based on the assumption (safe enough, indeed, for all present action) that men will not do unto others as they would be done by, that they do not love their neighbors as themselves, and that it is more blessed to receive than to give.

It is hard for us to visualize a state of society where the interest of others would have as much weight in determining conduct as our own interest. Yet it is doubtful whether a development of human sympathy which would be sufficient to overthrow all the laws of supply and demand would require any greater progress in altruism than has actually transpired in the last three or four centuries as represented by the general humanitarian movement.

In these days of flux and transformation, therefore, it is highly important to recognize that even those economic theories which have been regarded as most fundamental are really only relative, that the bases upon which they rest are at least conceivably susceptible of change. Yet it is plain enough that a quick adaptation of theories to fit changing conditions is the surest guarantee of peaceful progress and preventive of violent cataclysm, while premature changes are fatally obstructive. This is particularly true in the matter of the relation of labor to the other factors of production, which is one of the fundamental features of economic life, and one of the problems upon which economists have expended an untold amount of study. With labor disturbances on every hand, and wage problems thrusting themselves forward from every angle, it is well worth while to review the different wage theories which have commanded attention in the last one hundred years and particularly that which eventually dominated thought and practice down to the present time.

III

As an aid to achieving a suitable state of mind for studying wage theories it is well to remember that our present wage system, as a dominant industrial relation, is only a few generations old—a mere instant in the great span of human experience. It is of course impossible to fix an exact date for its commencement. It is sufficient to recognize that it has come into existence since the system of serfdom, which furnishes many contrasts to show how completely new the wage system is. The greatest contrast obviously is that between status and contract, but there are several other features which, individually or collectively, set the wage system entirely apart from any preceding industrial expedient.

The wage system, concisely stated, is one whereby the majority of the workers in gainful pursuits participate in product solely by their labor, which is sold to other parties, at terms fixed by a free contract, to be expended upon materials belonging to other parties, for the purpose of producing a product which at no time belongs either wholly or in part to the laborer, and over the processes of producing and disposing of which he has no control. Labor has about the same relation to the product as the coal thrown into the furnace of the power plant, or the lubricant poured into the oil-cups.

We are all inclined to feel that the institutions and social forms of our own day are the ultimate and final production of evolution. We admit, of course, that some amendments and reforms may come, but it is hard for us to realize, however assiduously we study history, that in a few generations many of our stable and cherished institutions may be supplanted by other forms as far removed from the present as the modern marriage procedure is from wife purchase or wife capture, or as far as democracy is from the absolute rule of divinely authorized monarchs. The great difficulty is to conceive of the coming of something the features of which we cannot predict. The feudal lords of the middle ages could not have predicted the modern wage system any more than the slave-owning landlords of Rome could have foreseen the feudal system. The fact that we of the present generation, thoroughly inoculated as we are with the individualistic-capitalistic system of the nineteenth century, cannot depict another system which will not only be different, but which will approach more nearly to the ideal of human justice, is no proof that such a system will not come. In point of fact, in accordance with the law of the accelerating rate of human evolution, changes of a given magnitude occur in ever shorter periods of time as the world rolls on.

Not only do the forms of today come to be looked upon as stable and unchangeable but they acquire a certain moral quality, so that those who predict (not to say advocate) a new order are looked upon as the enemies of society. This is very curiously illustrated by the extraordinary amount and variety of confusion which exists with reference to the various forms of radicalism which are rampant today, whereby one who advocates the nationalization of natural monopolies is classed with anarchists, and one who proposes to give women, married or single, equal financial responsibility with men is consigned to the same category as the advocate of free love. Any newspaper picked up at random will afford illustrations of the prevailing practice of classing one who advocates a different system of property rights as an enemy of the government. For example, an editorial in the New York Times, entitled "Enemies of the Republic," contains this sentence, "A gentleman who believes in the 'nationalization of railroads, coal mines, and perhaps other public utilities,' naturally shudders at deportations and has no sympathy with 'the antiradical policies' of Attorney General Palmer." It would be a tremendous shock to a good many people to be confronted with the proposition that socialism, as an economic system, whether desirable or not, probably could be completely installed in the United States without altering a single important feature of the machinery of government.

The wage theories of the past, present, and future,

therefore, can be adequately considered only by realizing that they are nothing more than explanations of the basis of remuneration of labor, and have to do with morals or governmental forms only as all social institutions have a certain interrelationship.

IV

In conformity with the facts, all the important wage theories of the nineteenth century started with the assumption that labor, or the laborer, is paid for his contribution out of funds belonging to some other individual or group of individuals. This relation has been variously expressed by saying that wages represent advances made to the laborer by the capitalist to enable the former to live while the process of production is being carried on, or as the return to the laborer of his share of the product. A complete wage theory must explain not only why wages must be paid, but how they come to be fixed at a certain amount. It is to this latter problem that economists have devoted most of their attention.

The wage theories which have predominated in economic thought from the beginning of the Industrial Revolution down to the present are four in number. The distinctive feature of each can be grasped without any undue digression into abstract theory or intricate analysis. The first to demand attention is the so-called "iron law" of wages, which held that general wages tend to be fixed at the minimum point necessary to enable the laborer to maintain himself in a reasonable degree of economic efficiency and rear a family to supply the laborers of the next generation. This was obviously a pessimistic theory, which harmonized well with the prevailing conception of economics as the "dismal science," and both rested upon and supported the Malthusian doctrine of population which was its contemporary. It also fitted in well with the social and economic conditions of the early nineteenth century.

The "iron law" was abandoned partly because it was visibly not absolutely true, there being at all times numerous laborers' families who were not living on the bare margin of subsistence, and partly, in all probability, because people did not wish to believe anything so horrible. It was succeeded by the "wage-fund" theory, which held that at the beginning of each year or season of production, the employers set aside a certain proportion of their capital to be paid as wages during the ensuing period. The amount of wages which each laborer received was the quotient derived by dividing the amount of money by the number of laborers. Increases in wages were thus made to depend on the increase of capital, and the limitation of population. This doctrine was very grateful to the capitalists, as it gave the credit for all positive progress to them through the accumulation of capital, and enabled them to answer complaints about low wages by saying that it was the laborers' own fault for having too many children. After long and heated discussion this theory was finally abandoned, because it had no real resemblance to the facts—no employer actually being in the habit of setting aside a certain amount of money for wages at the beginning of the year, or even determining in advance how much he intended to pay in wages during the year.

It was supplanted by the "productivity" theory, which maintained that wages are the return to labor of that part of the product which it has actually created, or in its most developed form, "wages are the discounted marginal product of labor." This was a very optimistic theory, corresponding to the improved conditions of labor, and particularly acceptable to the capitalist because it gave the laborer to understand that he was getting all he deserved, and that the only way to get more was to work harder and produce more. But in time this theory, like its predecessors, has weakened before the attacks of its critics because it cannot stand up beside the facts. There is nothing in this theory to show why wages differ so widely in a given industry in a given district, or why, as the result of a strike, wages may rise fifty per cent without any change in the price of the product, or why equally efficient women workers receive only half or two-thirds as much as men. It is, in truth, an ex post facto argument, one that begs the question. In the complicated processes of modern production no one has ever attempted to demonstrate what the actual contribution of each laborer is. It is sheer assumption that the laborer gets his contribution back, and from that assumption a deduction that what he contributes determines how much he gets.

Every widely accepted economic theory is almost certain to contain an element of truth, and to have a certain relation to the facts upon which it is supposed to rest. None of them is made out of whole cloth. Thus the theory which, beyond all question, best explains the amount of actual wages—the "bargain" theory—takes something from each of the others, particularly the "iron law" and the "productivity" theory. These two theories are very illuminating if considered not as complete explanations of wages, but merely as stating respectively the minimum and maximum limits between which wages must necessarily range. It is clear that over a long period of time wages cannot fall below the minimum of subsistence, else the number of laborers would decline and the competition for those who remained would raise their wages. It is equally clear that capitalists cannot continuously return to laborers more than their product, for this would bankrupt industry. But between the limits fixed by the "iron law" and the "productivity" theory there is an area of undefined extent over which wages range in response to factors not accounted for by any of the older theories. Within these two extremes the amount which is paid for any unit of labor is the result of a genuine bargain, just as in the case of any other commodity, except that the market conditions are more varied and imponderable than in the case of any other commodity, involving all sorts of conditions of intelligence, foresight, knowledge, need, sympathy, personal relations, venturesomeness, and everything else which goes to make up an individual's economic situation. This is the theory to which any practical employer would subscribe. He knows that he buys his labor just as he buys his coal, or his oil, or his raw material.

The laborers have always fought against the bargain theory of wages. They have vigorously objected to considering labor a commodity, and court decisions have been invoked to establish the point. They have insisted that a man should receive some especial consideration from the fact of his being a man, and that his productive capacity should not be thrown into the open market like so much inert matter. But these protestations have been of no avail. Whatever the economists might have been deciding as to theory, we have in practice said to the laborer, "You are worth just what we can get you for. Your capacity is subject to economic laws just like any other element in production. Your standard of living, the size of your family, your hopes and ideals have nothing to do with it. Your value is strictly a scarcity value, and you may expect to be paid just what your place can be filled for and no more." Departures from this procedure, which in all candor have occurred in countless thousands of cases, are merely deviations from the theory indulged in by individual employers who choose to be actuated by other principles than economic law. And any employer who habitually pays more than the accepted market rate of wages is almost certain to incur the enmity and condemnation of his class. This is particularly true in the case of domestic service, where the relations of serfdom still survive to a marked extent. Mrs. Jones, who is clever enough to secure a maid for a dollar less than her neighbors, wins the admiration and envy of those neighbors, while Mrs. Brown, who pays her maid a dollar more than the current rate, gets herself disliked. The characteristic attitude of the orthodox nineteenth century school of economics was forcibly expressed by one of its most brilliant spokesmen, William Graham Sumner, in the contemptuous scorn which he directed against the very idea of a "Menschenwurdiges Dasein."

V

The modern industrial unrest signalizes labor's eventual acceptance of the bargain theory as the correct interpretation of the actual facts of the remuneration of labor during the nineteenth century, and simultaneously registers a protest against those facts. This protest takes two forms. In its first form, labor accepts the bargain theory unreservedly and proposes to carry it to its logical application. Labor's reply is, in effect, "Very well, if we are worth just what we can be got for, we will proceed to show you just how high that figure may be raised. If wages are to be fixed by an unyielding competition, we will carry our end of that competition to the limit." This form of protest is represented by the trade union movement. Having been taught by long and bitter experience how unequal are the terms of the wage bargain when the laborer dickers as an individual with the employer, laborers have learned to combine, and are only beginning to learn how great is their power if the combination can be perfected.

It must be confessed that labor has been a thorough, though perhaps slow, student in the school of economic bargaining. The devices and expedients which it has developed are appalling in their devilish ingenuity. And the moral indignation expressed by many people with respect to the consciencelessness and general depravity of modern labor is, even while justified, grimly amusing. We are told that "this overweening greed, this limitation of product, this insatiate desire for advancement, this indifference to the profits of industry are intolerably unsocial." To be sure they are. But so were many of the methods of capital from which labor learned the lessons which it is now putting into application. All's fair in war.

The second form of protest is represented by the extremely radical economic doctrine that there can be no satisfactory economic conditions as long as one class of producers is paid by another class of producers, in other words, as long as the relation of master and servant persists in the economic field. "Wage-slavery must go." Some form of cooperation must be devised whereby the two basic factors of production, capital (including land) and labor, shall be on terms of perfect equality. Of course there is also the ultra radical element, represented by Syndicalism and the I. W. W., which demands a complete reversal, and the placing of all power in the hands of labor as a class.

The actual course of events, however, is almost always found in the mean, not in the extremes, and the Syndicalist ideal is no more likely to be realized in the future than is the individualistic-capitalistic system to be perpetuated.

All indications point to the conclusion that the days of the old bargain system of wages and the facts that permitted it are numbered. For reasons which it is not necessary to enumerate labor has acquired a solidarity, a power, and a self-conscious strength which will never permit of the restoration of the old conditions of bargaining. The pious protestations that the interests of capital and labor are identical are now recognized for the pitiful fallacies that they are. Any one who gets the least insight into the economic system of the past century knows that the interests of capital and labor are diametrically opposed, and always must be as long as that system persists. Of course in a general and rather remote way both capital and labor are interested that production should be as ample as possible. But the direct and immediate problem is how much of a product that belongs to one party the other party can secure as his remuneration. This is the thing that vitally concerns the laborer. He will take his chances on there always being product enough to pay him any wage which he may be able to extort from his employer.

There can be little question that at the present time labor is more unscrupulous, selfish, reckless, irresponsible, and generally unsocial than capital. What else is to be expected from labor's training and opportunities—especially when it has its innings. The one who has the upper hand can afford to be arrogant. And on the other hand, there is no more significant sign of the times than the eagerness of capital, grown most conspicuous within the past half dozen years, to placate and win public opinion.

As long as A hires B to help produce a product which belongs to A, there will always be an opposition of interest between the two as to how much of the product is to be turned over to B as his compensation. When the conflict is multiplied into nation-wide production, it becomes a matter of such stupendous proportions and such unmitigated evils that the general public, the party of ultimate interest, cannot tolerate its indefinite continuance. The bargain system of wages under the conditions of the nineteenth century was intolerable because the terms of the conflict were so unequal. The gains of labor during that century are perhaps to be credited as much to humanitarian violations of supposed economic law as to the capacity of labor to win things for itself under the operation of that law. The bargain system of wages in the twentieth century is also intolerable, but because the parties have become so nearly equal in power that the general public suffers from the fierceness of the unending strife. One of the penalties we must pay for political democracy is the abandonment of industrial autocracy. We cannot give the great mass of the people education, free thought, free speech, free assemblage, and a free press, and expect them to remain contentedly in a state of economic subordination.

VI

What the solution will be no one can predict with certainty. Those who are concerned that the transition should be by orderly evolution rather than by revolution, and who have the intelligence to help direct social currents should devote themselves soberly to working out a system which will both harmonize with the new economic forms which are most likely to arise, and which will help those forms to come into being by preparing the general public to understand and accept them.

There seem to be two main possibilities, either some method of actually evaluating the contribution of each laborer so that the return in wages may be demonstrably equitable, or else some entirely new system of relationship between capital and labor. The former problem seems almost incapable of solution. Modern production is so complicated and infinitesimally subdivided, that while each minute operation is absolutely essential to the whole, it is impossible to determine its relative importance and value. Even in so relatively simple a matter as the making of ready-made clothes the process is broken up into standardized operations. One man spends all his time making lapels, another pocket flaps, another buttonholes, etc. Who can say what part of the value of a fifty dollar coat is represented by the pocket flap?

One of the foremost economists of this country, in an article published a few years ago, cited the case of a certain factory which had declined from a long period of profitable operation into one of absolute loss. Nobody could discover what the trouble was. As a last resort the superintendent was dismissed and a new man put in his place. The new incumbent took no drastic action, but spent his time wandering about the plant in an apparently aimless way, but with his eyes wide open. Finally, down in one of the initial stages of production, he found two men who were soldiering on their job, and thereby holding up the entire plant. He dismissed them, put two faithful men in their places, and production at once bounded ahead to profitable proportions. The query with which the author pointed his moral was, "Wasn't this superintendent worth the fifty thousand dollars the company had to pay him?" The answer is obviously affirmative. But another question insistently intrudes itself, "How much was that piece of work worth, upon the faithful performance of which the entire prosperity of the plant depended? Does a man who can detect poor work deserve any greater pay than the man who does good work?"

Last summer 1,114 policemen went on strike in Boston for something better than $3.66 per day in wages. During the first day that they were off duty damage was done because of their absence estimated at $300,000. How much are a policeman's services worth per day? A little later from 30,000 to 40,000 longshoremen went on strike in New York. The loss caused by their idleness was estimated at more than $1,500,000 per day. What is the value to the community of the daily labor of a dockhand?

The simple fact is that under the complex conditions of modern life we are all infinitely dependent on each other. The contribution of many of the humblest workers is virtually indispensable, and therefore of immeasurable value in itself. It has doubtless been largely because we could not determine the actual worth of a service that we have had to fall back on the scarcity valuation, and say that the price of a job is measured by the sum for which somebody can be found to do it. It has accordingly come about that those pieces of work for which the greatest number of people are fitted, which are nevertheless often the most necessary and essential, are regarded as worthy of the lowest pay. Just because a man has qualities which are common to the great mass of humanity, even though they are the most necessary qualities, he must content himself with a minimum remuneration. Abraham Lincoln is reported to have said that the Lord must love common people—he made so many of them. The Lord may love common people, but the fact that he made so many of them is no evidence of it while the bargain system of wages prevails.

Even though a method could be worked out for evaluating the contributions of laborers, it would hardly be more than a temporary solution of the labor problem, For the problem is much more than one of wages. To assume that the ambition of the laborer can be permanently satisfied by increases in wages, however munificent, is entirely to misread the signs of the times. Labor will be satisfied, and a stable adjustment reached, only when labor as a body (it usually helps to interpret economic problems to think of the aggregate "labor" rather than of individual laborers) attains a degree of dignity, responsibility, independence, and interest equal to that of capital.

It would be vain to try to work out in advance the exact steps by which this result is to be achieved, or the definite lineaments of the new system. Neither should we expect the change to occur immediately or all at once. The natural way of progress is by successive steps in a given direction. Some of our industrial plants which have provided for the election of labor members on their boards of directors are unquestionably moving in harmony with the developments of the future. They are anticipating in a small way the time when labor will share with capital in both the control of production and the ownership of the product.

The stock objection to such schemes as have been proposed in the past for labor's participation in the gains of industry, such as profit sharing, has been that, in all logic and fairness, if labor is to share in the gains it ought also to share in the losses, but that labor is not in a position to assume the risk of loss. This is perfectly true of the individual laborer, but it is not true of labor in the mass. The enormous union funds revealed by recent strikes show how large a surplus labor can make available for purposes which it believes in. Possibly in the future some form of insurance will be devised whereby labor's risks may be widely distributed, and reduced to proportions bearable by the individual laborer. Or some form of labor investment may be devised which will do for labor what the limited-liability joint-stock company did for capital.

It is not necessary for peaceful progress that we should foresee far in advance what the new forms will be. Nor is it desirable that we should attempt to hasten their coming prematurely. To do so would in fact be disastrous. What is necessary is that every thinking man and woman should recognize the transient character of the best economic theories, and should realize that those who impede progress by clinging to an outgrown theory must share the responsibility for any violent upheaval which may come, equally with those who try to force the adoption of new and untried devices before the time is ripe for them.

ACKNOWLEDGMENT

Grateful acknowledgment is hereby tendered to the publishers of the magazines in which the essays included in this volume originally appeared, and thanks for their kind permisson to reprint them in the present form. In some cases the title has been changed; in others it has remained the same. The complete list as originally printed is presented below.

Chaper I

But You Can't Have Both . . . . Harper's, March, 1934

Chapter II

The Fallacy of Profits . . . . Harper's, February, 1932

Chapter III

The Land-hunger Urge to War . . . . Forum, September, 1925

Chapter IV

The Deeper Significance of Prohibition . . . . Virginia Quarterly Review, April, 1928

Chapter V

The Matter with Teaching . . . . Educational Review, December, 1919

ACKNOWLEDGMENT

Chapter VI

Business as an Institution . . . .
. . . . American Sociological Review, February, 1937

Chapter VII

Machines Don't Buy Goods . . . .
. . . . . . Virginia Quarterly Review, January, 1931

Chapter VIII

Lies, Damned Lies, and Statistics . . . .
. . . . Unpopular Review, April, 1915

Chapter IX

Battling Impulses . . . .
. . . . . . Virginia Quarterly Review, October, 1926

Chapter X

Exit the Gospel of Work . . . .
. . . . Harper's, April, 1931

Chapter XI

Will the Wage System Last . . . .
. . . . . . Unpartisan Review, June-September, 1920

INDEX

Note. In many listings the singular includes the plural or vice versa

INDEX

INDEX

INDEX

INDEX